IFIP Advances in Information and Communication Technology 531

IFIP – The International Federation for Information Processing

IFIP was founded in 1960 under the auspices of UNESCO, following the first World Computer Congress held in Paris the previous year. A federation for societies working in information processing, IFIP's aim is two-fold: to support information processing in the countries of its members and to encourage technology transfer to developing nations. As its mission statement clearly states:

> *IFIP is the global non-profit federation of societies of ICT professionals that aims at achieving a worldwide professional and socially responsible development and application of information and communication technologies.*

IFIP is a non-profit-making organization, run almost solely by 2500 volunteers. It operates through a number of technical committees and working groups, which organize events and publications. IFIP's events range from large international open conferences to working conferences and local seminars.

The flagship event is the IFIP World Computer Congress, at which both invited and contributed papers are presented. Contributed papers are rigorously refereed and the rejection rate is high.

As with the Congress, participation in the open conferences is open to all and papers may be invited or submitted. Again, submitted papers are stringently refereed.

The working conferences are structured differently. They are usually run by a working group and attendance is generally smaller and occasionally by invitation only. Their purpose is to create an atmosphere conducive to innovation and development. Refereeing is also rigorous and papers are subjected to extensive group discussion.

Publications arising from IFIP events vary. The papers presented at the IFIP World Computer Congress and at open conferences are published as conference proceedings, while the results of the working conferences are often published as collections of selected and edited papers.

IFIP distinguishes three types of institutional membership: Country Representative Members, Members at Large, and Associate Members. The type of organization that can apply for membership is a wide variety and includes national or international societies of individual computer scientists/ICT professionals, associations or federations of such societies, government institutions/government related organizations, national or international research institutes or consortia, universities, academies of sciences, companies, national or international associations or federations of companies.

More information about this series at http://www.springer.com/series/6102

Lynette Drevin · Marianthi Theocharidou (Eds.)

Information Security Education – Towards a Cybersecure Society

11th IFIP WG 11.8 World Conference, WISE 11
Held at the 24th IFIP World Computer Congress, WCC 2018
Poznan, Poland, September 18–20, 2018
Proceedings

 Springer

Editors
Lynette Drevin 🆔
North-West University
Potchefstroom
South Africa

Marianthi Theocharidou 🆔
European Commission Joint
 Research Centre
Ispra
Italy

ISSN 1868-4238   ISSN 1868-422X (electronic)
IFIP Advances in Information and Communication Technology
ISBN 978-3-319-99733-9   ISBN 978-3-319-99734-6 (eBook)
https://doi.org/10.1007/978-3-319-99734-6

Library of Congress Control Number: 2018952563

This Springer imprint is published by the registered company Springer Nature Switzerland AG
The registered company address is: Gewerbestrasse 11, 6330 Cham, Switzerland

Preface

This volume contains the papers presented at the 11th World Conference on Information Security Education (WISE 11) held during September 18–20, 2018, in Poznan, Poland, in conjunction with the 24th IFIP World Computer Congress. WISE 11 was organized by the IFIP Working Group 11.8, which is an international group of people from academia, government, and private organizations who volunteer their time and effort to increase knowledge in the very broad field of information security through education. WG11.8 has worked to increase information security education and awareness for almost two decades.

This year, WG11.8 organized the 11th conference of a successful series under the theme "Towards a Cybersecure Society." We received 25 submissions from around the world. Each submission was blind reviewed by at least three international Program Committee members. The committee decided to accept 11 full papers. The acceptance rate for the papers is thus 44%.

In line with this year's theme, several additional events on cybersecurity took place during the three days of the conference. On the second day of the conference, the "SecTech Cybersecurity Curriculum Workshop" was organized by the SecTech Project Partnership. The following day, a new "TC11.8 Work Group on Cyber Ranges and Cyber Challenges" was discussed based on a proposal by the Norwegian University of Science and Technology and the Norwegian Defence University College. Both events are described in detail in the following section of this preface. S. E. Goodman (chair), S. Furnell, R. von Solms, and M. Bishop formed a panel discussing the topic of "Building National Cybersecurity Workforces." The panel highlighted challenges, such as how to estimate the size and make-up of national cyber security workforces based on needs, how to characterize such workforces, and how to achieve balance between employing organizations' priorities and national needs. The panel also addressed how such challenges may differ across a range of nations as well as the role of educational institutions to stimulate supply and demand. We would like to thank all the panelists and workshop organizers for their contribution to the conference.

This conference took place thanks to the support and commitment of many individuals. First, we would like to thank all TC-11 members for continually giving us the opportunity to serve the working group and organize the WISE conferences. Our sincere appreciation also goes to the members of the Program Committee, to the external reviewers, and to the authors who trusted us with their intellectual work.

We are grateful for the support of WISE11.8 Officers L. Futcher, M. Bishop, N. Miloslavskaya, and E. Moore. Finally, we would like to thank the local organizers for the support and especially the IFIP WCC 2018 General Congress co-chairs R. Slowinski and L. Strous for the collaboration. For the preparation of this volume, we sincerely thank E. Siebert-Cole and our publisher Springer for their assistance.

July 2018

Lynette Drevin
Marianthi Theocharidou

Organization

WISE11 Conference Chair

Lynn Futcher   Nelson Mandela University, South Africa

WISE11 Program Chair

Lynette Drevin   North-West University, South Africa

WISE11 Conference Secretariat

Matt Bishop   University of California, Davis, USA

WISE11 Publications Chair

Marianthi Theocharidou   European Commission, Joint Research Centre, Italy

WISE11 Local and Logistics Chair

Natalia Miloslavskaya   National Research Nuclear University MEPhI, Russia

WISE11 Web Chair

Erik Moore   Regis University, Colorado, USA

Program Committee

Maria Bada   University of Oxford, UK
Matt Bishop   University of California, Davis, USA
William Caelli   IISEC Pty Ltd, Australia
Nathan Clarke   University of Plymouth, UK
Jun Dai   California State University, Sacramento, USA
Melissa Dark   Purdue University, USA
Tamara Denning   University of Utah, USA
Lynette Drevin   North-West University, South Africa
Steven Furnell   Plymouth University, UK
Lynn Futcher   Nelson Mandela University, South Africa
Roberto Gallo   University of Campinas, Brazil
Seymour Goodman   Georgia Institute of Technology, USA
Ram Herkanaido   Plymouth University, UK
Lech Janczewski   The University of Auckland, New Zealand
Borka Jerman-Blazic   University of Ljubljana, Slovenia

Audun Josang	University of Oslo, Norway
Suresh Kalathur	Boston University, USA
Christos Kalloniatis	University of the Aegean, Greece
Vasilios Katos	Bournemouth University, UK
Sokratis Katsikas	Center for Cyber and Information Security, NTNU, Norway
Siddharth Kaza	Towson University, USA
Andrea Kolberger	University of Applied Sciences Upper Austria, Austria
Elmarie Kritzinger	UNISA, South Africa
Hennie Kruger	North-West University, South Africa
Costas Lambrinoudakis	University of Piraeus, Greece
Javier Lopez	University of Malaga, Spain
Herbert Mattord	Kennesaw State University, USA
Vashek Matyas	Masaryk University, Czech Republic
Natalia Miloslavskaya	National Research Nuclear University MEPhI, Russia
Stig Mjolsnes	Norwegian University of Science and Technology, Norway
Erik Moore	Regis University, Colorado, USA
Kara Nance	University of Alaska Fairbanks, USA
Jason Nurse	University of Kent, UK
Ruxandra Olimid	Norwegian University of Science, Norway Technology and University of Bucharest, Romania
Jacques Ophoff	University of Cape Town, South Africa
Allen Parrish	United States Naval Academy, USA
Günther Pernul	Universität Regensburg, Germany
Carlos Rieder	isec ag, Switzerland
Chien-Chung Shen	University of Delaware, USA
Marianthi Theocharidou	European Commission Joint Research Centre, Italy
Kerry-Lynn Thomson	Nelson Mandela University, South Africa
Alexander Tolstoy	National Research Nuclear University MEPhI, Russia
Ismini Vasileiou	Plymouth University, UK
Rossouw Von Solms	Nelson Mandela University, South Africa
Edgar Weippl	SBA Research, Austria
Susanne Wetzel	Stevens Institute of Technology, USA
Stephen D. Wolthusen	Royal Holloway, University of London, UKNorwegian University of Science and Technology, Norway
Louise Yngstrom	Stockholm University and Royal Institute of Technology, Sweden
Sergey Zapechnikov	National Research Nuclear University MEPhI, Russia

Additional Reviewers

Böhm, Fabian

Contents

Information Security Learning Techniques

A Design for a Collaborative Make-the-Flag Exercise

Matt Bishop[✉]

University of California at Davis, Davis, CA, USA
mabishop@ucdavis.edu

Abstract. Many people know how to compromise existing systems, and capture-the-flag contests are increasing this number. There is a dearth of people who know how to design and build secure systems. A collaborative contest to build secure systems to meet specific goals—a "make-the-flag" exercise—could encourage more people to participate in cybersecurity exercises, and learn how to design and build secure systems. This paper presents a generic design for such an exercise. It explores the goals, organization, constraints, and rules. It also discusses preparations and how to run the exercise and evaluate the results. Several variations are also presented.

1 Introduction

Cybersecurity has become a major concern, and its lack a serious problem in society. Exacerbating this problem is the poor quality of software and systems, enabling attackers to exploit vulnerabilities that compromise security. This is a product of many things, including the economics of the marketplace [3,4] and a lack of programmers and system developers who understand how to craft programs and systems that meet a specific set of security requirements, as well as more generic robustness requirements.

In computer security curricula and competitions, a common exercise is to have students find flaws in existing systems. In some cases, the organizers of competitions make their own systems (such as DefCon's Clemency system [1]). The goal of these exercises and competitions (called "Capture-the-Flag" or "CTF" contests) is to teach students how to find and exploit vulnerabilities, thereby teaching them what to avoid doing.

A variant of these CTF competitions is to provide the contestants with an existing system that is known to have vulnerabilities. They are given some period of time, such as a month, to harden the system so that any vulnerabilities cannot be exploited, and all attempts to do so are recorded. The systems are then attacked by other teams or a "red team" and the contestants are given points for the attacks they have blocked. These "Protect-the-Flag" ("PTF") competitions are more constructive than the CTF ones because the emphasis is on securing a system, not breaching it.

© IFIP International Federation for Information Processing 2018
Published by Springer Nature Switzerland AG 2018. All Rights Reserved
L. Drevin and M. Theocharidou (Eds.): WISE 2018, IFIP AICT 531, pp. 3–14, 2018.
https://doi.org/10.1007/978-3-319-99734-6_1

Consider the ultimate goal of security. It is to create systems that satisfy a specific set of requirements. The CTF competition focuses on showing an existing system fails to do this. A PTF competition focuses on protecting an existing but fundamentally non-secure system to prevent it from violating a set of security requirements. Neither of these do what a "secure system" is to do: demonstrate to some desired level of assurance that a system meets a set of specific requirements, including security requirements.

This suggests an alternate exercise in which the contestants design and implement a system to meet specific requirements, including security requirements. This exercise, a "Make-the-Flag" (MTF) exercise, has the teams work from the ground up to design and build a secure system, rather than work from the top down to take a system apart. Such a exercise would of necessity involve a special-purpose system because designing and implementing a general-purpose system from scratch would take too long. This shifts the focus to creating secure systems, thereby decreasing the problem of a lack of practitioners who can do that. It also forces students to pull together everything they have learned in computer science classes—software engineering, robust programming, networking, security, and so forth—to build a system that will be tested thoroughly for vulnerabilities. It will also encourage academic programs to put more emphasis on teaching this art of construction.

A second aspect of an MTF exercise is that it can be run collaboratively rather than competitively. This makes it attractive to people who either find competition distasteful or do not have confidence that they will score well on a competition. In the collaborative form, team members can support members of other teams as well as members of their own team. The teams compete against a set of requirements, and the evaluation of a team's effort results in a non-numeric report of the quality of their work. Thus, there is no high or low score. Of course, an MTF exercise can be run as a competition by providing numeric scores for the components of the evaluation; we shall return to this later.

In this paper, we explore how a collaborative MTF exercise might be organized and run.

2   Background

Traditional CTF competitions are exercises in which contestants set up systems containing a "flag," or indicator. The object of the competition is to capture as many flags from other teams' systems while preventing the capture of your flag. Scoring takes into account both the number of flags captured and the number of times the contestants' own flag has been captured.

Several versions of this basic format exist. MIT Lincoln Labs held a CTF contest for Boston-area universities with the goal of providing practical cybersecurity education [15]. They distributed the system as a virtual machine, encouraged the students to study it, and before the contest provided five lectures on various aspects of cybersecurity and vulnerabilities. The final lecture was a lab exercise in which students worked through various challenges using Google's Gruyere service [8]. The score for the exercise depended on defense, calculated as a weighted sum of confidentiality, integrity, and availability measures, and then combined with a weighted measure of offense, or the capture of other teams' flags. The organizers released two plug-ins, one near the beginning of the contest and the other near the end, that had to be added to the systems. Failure to do so diminished the availability score.

Every DefCon has a CTF contest. In one DefCon CTF contest, the "flag" was a data file, and a "capture" was defined as corrupting that file. So the goal was to corrupt as many opponent's data files as possible without allowing yours to be corrupted. Cowan's team used this to test their Immunix server [6].

The U.S. military schools run a PTF, the Cyber Defense Exercise (CDX), annually. In some competitions, the schools could choose their own network architectures and associated security architecture [10]. In another [2], each military school was given control of enterprise systems that were poorly managed. In all exercises, the systems were on an isolated, closed network. The teams had to identify vulnerabilities and ameliorate them as well as secure the networks, and do so within a given time and budget. The U.S. National Security Agency then provided a red team to attack, and that team used only publicly available exploits. The students were scored on their ability to keep services running in the face of attacks as well as their success in detecting the attacks and defending the systems. They also had to submit reports and respond to requests.

The Collegiate Cyber Defense Competition (CCDC) is a civilian CTF run the same way as the CDX [5,12]. The students are presented with a business environment, including a web server, email, and other services. It emphasizes the operational aspects of securing the network infrastructure, as well as solving business problems. A red team acts as adversary, with limits similar to those of the CDX red team. The CCDC has grown from a small competition among Texas schools to a U.S. national competition. The traditional edition of the International CTF Competition [14] also uses this scheme.

Vigna describes three versions of these exercises [13]. The Red Team/Blue Team exercise is essentially a CTF exercise, with one set of participants playing the role of attackers (Red Team) and the other playing the role of defenders (Blue Team). The CTF exercise again split the participants into two teams, with each team attacking the other team's system and detecting (not preventing) attacks on its system by the other team. Another exercise, called the Treasure Hunt, had two teams compete to complete given tasks in a specific period of time, and the competition was to do so first within that time.

The Cyber Security Exercise Workshop [7], sponsored by the U.S. National Science Foundation, considered four types of exercises: defensive exercises; small, internal CTF competitions; national CTF competitions; and semester-long CTF competitions. It described organizational and logistical issues in establishing a CTF cybersecurity exercise.

A perceptive paper [11] discussed ways to involve members of groups that are traditionally underrepresented in the cybersecurity field, such as females. The paper presented several ways to make cybersecurity competitions more attractive, and how to support the participation of these members. Interestingly, its scope was restricted to *competitions*; it did not consider collaboration at all.

Some of the CTF exercises require that the system be protected, which typically requires the design of configurations to harden the systems; in some cases, the contestants may have to write programs. The difference is that the focus of the MTF contest is to design and implement a system from the ground up as opposed to hardening something that exists. Further, the focus of this work is on collaboration.

3   The Make-the-Flag Exercise

An MTF exercise has several steps: organizing the contest, preparing the teams, running the exercise, and then evaluating the results. Doing so involves several groups.

- The *teams* are groups that are participating in the exercise. Their goal is to build a robust, secure system.
- The *managers* of the exercise set the requirements to be met, the components of the system to be used, and any additional constraints (such as when and for how long the exercise is to run, and who may participate).
- The *testers* test the systems at the end of the competition. They do not score the results numerically; instead, they provide written reports that can be given to the teams.
- The *judges* evaluate the results of the testing and of the exercise in general. They determine the effectiveness of each system based upon the this evaluation.

The managers and judges are together called the *organizers*, and the testers and judges are together called the *evaluators*.

Teams are not ranked against one another; instead, the systems are evaluated and the evaluation serves as the results. This emphasizes that the goal of this exercise is *cooperation*, not competition.

3.1   Organizing the Contest

In this step, the organizers meet to determine the goals and rules of the contest, and to organize themselves into the managers and judges.

Goals. The generic goals of the teams in an MTF exercise are twofold. First, develop a system that meets the requirements stated by the organizers. Second, ensure the system is robust, in the sense that generic attacks such as buffer overflows do not result in the system entering a compromised state.

Each contest also has more specific goals for the teams to meet. The organizers must decide what those goals are, and to what level they are to be specified. One approach is to present an objective, leaving teams to determine how best to meet it.

Example. The objective of this MTF exercise is to develop a small computer system that will manage a set of street lights on corners. Lights opposite one another are to be paired so they are always the same color. When one set is red (stop), the other set is green (go). The computer is to be managed through an Internet connection. ■

Rules. Given this objective, the teams must develop a set of requirements, show that a system meeting the requirements will meet the objective, and then develop the system. In doing so, they will also have to develop the necessary network protocols, command interface and language, and output protocols. Further, they must document these thoroughly enough so that people who were not the developers can configure and use the system. This approach thus offers the teams the maximum degree of freedom, while teaching them to document their interfaces and other external features of their system thoroughly enough for the evaluators to be able to use and to test their system.

The disadvantage is that each system developed in the contest is likely to have completely different interfaces. This makes the utility of the system more difficult to evaluate, especially if it is to be used in a particular environment. It also increases the time needed for thorough testing. In this case, the objective should include some details of inputs and outputs:

Example. The objective of this MTF exercise is to develop a small computer system that will manage a set of street lights on corners. Lights opposite one another are to be paired so they are always the same color. When one set is red (stop), the other set is green (go). The lights will be connected using the connector described in the addendum, and controlled using the protocol described there. The computer will accept inputs as described in the addendum, both over the network and from a command-line interface. ■

The addendum specifies the interfaces with the external environment, limiting what the computer can do but providing a standard interface for all teams to implement. Thus, they need not document the protocols or the command-line interface unless they add extensions, in which case those must be documented.

An exercise to construct a simple firewall gives another example of a very detailed set of requirements,

Example. The objective of this MTF exercise is to develop a simple firewall system that will accept or reject network packets based on rulesets. The managers have devised a little language for the ruleset. The specific requirements are:

1. The system must receive packets on one network interface.
2. The system must either forward the packets over another interface, or discard them, as dictated by the ruleset.
3. The system must accept rulesets written in the RULESET language; see the addendum.
4. The system must provide a command-line interface; see the addendum.

5. Once started, the system will run until a SHUTDOWN command is entered at the user interface or until powered down. ∎

In addition, the managers provide the addendum describing the RULESET language and the command-line interface.

In addition to meeting the requirements and objective, the teams must develop systems that are robust in the sense that they will handle error conditions in a reasonable manner—providing informative error messages, rejecting the bad input, and taking other actions as appropriate. For example, if the traffic light system receives inputs telling it to turn all lights green, the system should reject that input; if something fails, then the system should have the lights fail safe, that is, all either turn red or enter some other specified state. If the firewall system has too many rules, it should inform the user of the overflow, and reject the excess rules; it should not simply ignore all rules.[1]

Constraints. The organizers must also decide on other aspects of the exercise. The first is the time for the contest: when it starts and how long the teams have. The second is what equipment, and other financial limits, are necessary for each team, and how it will be procured.

Time is a complex constraint. Some team members will be students and their schedules will require attention to schoolwork, especially when examinations are being given. Similarly, non-students will have job-related constraints. So the organizers should aim for a time that minimizes the disruption of the schedules of the expected team members. It will not be possible to accommodate everyone's schedule, but the organizers should position the contest so the team members can devote maximum effort to the contest.

The financial constraints are also critical, and simulate real-world constraints. The simplest method for handling them is for the organizers to procure a set of hardware and software, and loan each team what is needed. If the objective allows the use of commodity hardware (such as PCs), then the organizers can expect the teams to have their own available, although the organizers should have some financial aid available for teams who have neither the equipment nor the support of their institution to purchase the equipment. The organizers should make any additional constraints, financial and otherwise, explicit *before* the exercise starts.

Organization. At this point, the organizers need to assemble the teams. This is a recruiting and marketing issue, and techniques similar to those used in CTF contests should work. Word-of-mouth, reaching out to faculty in cybersecurity programs, to cybersecurity clubs, and other groups will be helpful, as will the organizers determine an enticing set of prizes. Also, the organizers should seek industry and government sponsorship and support, because those groups are attempting to improve the state of commercial and non-commercial software and

---

[1] This is from an incident where the author and his students were testing a firewall. The bug was quickly fixed.

systems, and so should be happy to support such a contest. Their support will encourage teams to form, because the contest will be a showcase for their talents. Indeed, as with many CTF exercises, once the MTF exercise runs successfully a few times, little recruiting will be necessary.

3.2   Preparing the Teams

Once the teams are organized, they must learn the rules and objectives of the MTF contest. The organizers must be explicit is what is, and is not, allowed. For example, must the teams use the equipment that the organizers supply, or may the teams use their own equipment. If the latter, the organizers need to specify any constraints—for example, that a USB-3 port will be required to connect some specialized peripherals, or that the system is to use particular drivers that the organizers will supply. Given that many MTF contests will require the teams to develop special-purpose systems, whether the teams must develop their own system supervisor or whether they can use a commodity system like picoLinux or Windows CE must also be specified.

An interesting question is whether cross-team collaboration should be encouraged. As this is not a competition, cross-team collaboration may provide the teams with fresh ideas. It also improves the assurance aspect of the systems, as teams can co-operate to test each others' systems and point out problems that would otherwise not be discovered until the testing phase of the exercise. The organizers should make any limits clear to all.

Another question is whether there are constraints on software development. The organizers can specify that a particular language, set of libraries, or development environment is to be used, as well as a particular software development methodology. If they do this the organizers must also determine how the teams are to demonstrate that they have used the specified methodology and environment. In some sense, such a detailed specification would violate the purpose of the contest. If the goal is to encourage teams to meet the requirements, then *how* they meet those requirements should be left up to the team. As the cliché says, "You can tell me what to do or how to do it. If you want to tell me both, *you* do it!"

Once the organizers have presented the objectives, requirements, and rules, undoubtedly teams will have questions. The more clarity the organizers can provide at the beginning of the contest, the better prepared the teams will be to meet the objectives. The organizers should emphasize the non-competitive nature of the exercise by making the questions and answers available to all teams.

It will be critical to emphasize the collaborative nature of the exercise, and ensure the teams realize the only competition is against themselves—they build the requisite system, provide evidence it does what it is supposed to, and have the system do so in the face of both regular and malicious testing. Every team that does this wins. Conceivable, *all* teams could win; similarly, all teams can lose. But team A winning does not interfere in any way with team B winning.

3.3 Running the Exercise

This part is divided into two phases. The first is the development phase; the second, the testing phase.

During the development phase, the teams design and implement their systems in accordance with the rules. Their ultimate goal is to convince the evaluators that their system meets the stated requirements and objectives. Accumulating assurance evidence—evidence that the system meets the requirements provided by the application of specific techniques such as requirements tracing—is part of the way to show this.

The organizers may define both the form and the content of the documentation of the development process. The manner in which that content is gathered is up to the teams. What does matter is how they write the documentation. Documentation that organizes the methods used to gather assurance evidence, that describes how those methods were applied and the results of their application, will provide information that customers—here, the evaluators – can use to determine how well the system meets its requirements. The documentation also provides information that the evaluators can use to assess the interfaces through which people communicate with the system.

Part of gathering assurance evidence is testing. The documentation needs to describe the testing in enough detail so others can reproduce the tests and verify the results. In some cases, repeating a test may produce different results; for example, a race condition may occur infrequently, so one test will trigger it but others will not. These test results should be identified as occurring intermittently, so the evaluators understand that the results of repeated tests will vary. The developers should explain why this occurs.

Undoubtedly, in some cases the developers will not be able to conduct all the tests they think of. The tests that are not run should still be described, so the evaluators know what the developers would do with more time.

The description of each test should follow the concepts used in the flaw hypothesis methodology's flaw hypothesis generation step [9]. Each test attempts to validate a hypothesis or claim. That claim is to be stated, and the testing methodology shown to demonstrate or refute the claim. The developers then state the results, noting anything unexpected, and state whether the results support the claim.

When the time period for the exercise ends, the developers submit their system and documentation to the evaluators.

3.4 Evaluating the Results

The job of the evaluators is to determine whether the system meets the requirements and objectives of the exercise, as well as other factors such as usability and robustness.

The evaluator can use techniques such as source code analysis to look at the quality of the system. In some cases, the exercise will specify use procedures; in others, the developers will need to design these procedures to enable the system to meet its requirements. In either case, as security is a product of the system and how and under what conditions it is to be used, the evaluators need to consider these procedures as part of the security of the system.

The teams submit documentation that assembles assurance evidence, and the methods used to collect it. The reason is to provide a road map for the evaluators. The evaluators look at what was tested, and possibly repeat the validation steps in that document. The evaluators also look at what was *not* tested to find areas that the teams either did not think of or did not test.

The evaluation itself is qualitative, not quantitative. Knowing one system scored 5 out of a possible 10 points, and another 7 out of 10, says nothing about the significance of the difference. The causes of the ratings may speak to the same aspect of the system, in which case the difference in scores may be significant, or they may speak to different aspects of the system, in which case the difference in scores is not significant. Hence a qualitative description will provide information that the team members can learn from.

4   Variations on This Theme

Variations of the exercise proposed here provide other benefits. The exercise can be framed as a competition, in which case a quantitative evaluation is necessary. The teams can also act as testers to provide preliminary feedback before the evaluation phase of the exercise.

Cooperative Competition. Many institutions and groups desire a ranking of results, as well as (or rather than) a detailed evaluation. This exercise can be changed into a competition by the judges assigning team rankings based upon their evaluation. If the organizers wish to base the rankings on specific numbers of points, they should assign points to each requirement, and a general point count to "robustness." The testers would evaluate each aspect of the requirements and robustness to which points were assigned, and the judges would determine the number of points to be assigned.

The critical aspect here is that the teams receive more than just a numeric ranking or point score. They need to learn what problems the testers found, because problems teach more than success.

Teams as Testers. To give experience in testing systems, the teams themselves can act as testers.[2]

One way to do this is to give the teams access to all systems during the testing step. Then each team would test the systems, and provide reports to both the team that developed the system and the judges. The test reports would describe the tests conducted in sufficient detail that others can reproduce them. The judges would then evaluate the systems based on the test reports. If the teams test the system, the judges should also evaluate the test reports themselves.

---

[2] Thanks to Dan Ragsdale for this suggestion.

A second way eliminates the students as evaluators. The MTF exercise is structured into three rounds, in the following order:

1. *Development round.* In this round, the teams build their systems. This round proceeds as the MTF exercise described above.
2. *Test round.* In this round, the teams are given access to one another's systems. They then carry out the testing. As in the other version, the test reports are made available to the other teams and the evaluators.
3. *Repair round.* The teams fix the problems found in the previous round.

After the third round, the testers, and the judges then evaluate both the results of the testing and the reports from the test round. The results of the exercise depend on both the system's quality and the quality of each team's testing.

5   Conclusion

This paper explored an alternative to a traditional CTF contest. This alternative is constructive, in that the goal is to create a secure system rather than find holes in an existing system. While the latter is instructive and necessary to teaching students how to "think like an attacker," the former gives the students experience in creating hardened systems. It allows them to practice the principles of secure development, implementation, and evaluation.

The other aspect is an emphasis on collaboration rather than competition. CTF exercises can be intimidating, particularly to those who have never participated in one, or who feel themselves overmatched by more experienced players. The Make-the-Flag exercise encourages teamwork that helps team members learn from one another and from a qualitative evaluation of their work. In collaborative exercises, there is no penalty for aiding another team, so the learning can cross team boundaries. This type of exercise will be appealing to those who are not by nature competitive.

One could also picture a CTF contest run collaboratively. Such an exercise would follow the pattern of the CCDC or CDX, except that the teams would work together to help each other secure their systems. They would compete as one group against the red team testers, and their goal would be to minimize the success of that team. The scoring or evaluation would require the red team to keep careful track of what they tried, and what worked and what did not, so the other teams could receive a detailed evaluation of each of their systems. Such a framing would allow teams to try different approaches and see which ones worked best, without the fear of "losing" or "winning" due to these different implementations.

Competitive exercises, and exercises emphasizing attacks, have their place. But many potential cybersecurity students are dissuaded from following that field because of this emphasis. Emphasizing collaboration and construction may draw them in, to the benefit of the field, the profession, and the community. It is an idea worth trying.

Acknowledgements. Thanks to Dan Ragsdale of Texas A&M University and Kara Nance of the Virginia Polytechnic Institute and State University for helpful discussions. The author gratefully acknowledges support of the National Science Foundation under Grant Numbers DGE-1303211 and OAC-1739025, and a gift from Intel Corporation. Any opinions, findings, and conclusions or recommendations expressed in this material are those of the author(s) and do not necessarily reflect the views of the National Science Foundation, Intel Corporation or the University of California at Davis.

References

1. The cLEMCy architecture, July 2017. https://blog.legitbs.net/2017/07/the-clemency-architecture.html
2. Adams, W.J., Gavas, E., Lacey, T., Leblanc, S.: Collective views of the NSA/CSS cyber defense exercise on curricula and learning objectives. In: Proceedings of the Second Workshop on Cyber Security Experimentation and Test. USENIX Association, Berkeley, August 2009. https://www.usenix.org/legacy/event/cset09/tech/full_papers/adams.pdf
3. Anderson, R.: Why information security is hard–an economic perspective. In: Proceedings of the 17th Annual Computer Security Applications Conference. IEEE Computer Society, Los Alamitos, December 2001. https://doi.org/10.1109/ACSAC.2001.991552
4. Anderson, R., Moore, T.: Information security economics – and beyond. In: Menezes, A. (ed.) CRYPTO 2007. LNCS, vol. 4622, pp. 68–91. Springer, Heidelberg (2007). https://doi.org/10.1007/978-3-540-74143-5_5
5. Conklin, A.: The use of a collegiate cyber defense competition in information security education. In: Proceedings of the Second Annual Conference on Information Security Curriculum Development, pp. 16–18. ACM, New York, September 2005. https://doi.org/10.1145/1107622.1107627
6. Cowan, C., Arnold, S., Beattie, S., Wright, C., Viega, J.: DefCon capture the flag: defending vulnerable code from intense attack. In: Proceedings of the 2003 DARPA Information Survivability Conference and Exposition. IEEE Computer Society, Los Alamitos, April 2003. https://doi.org/10.1109/DISCEX.2003.1194878
7. Hoffman, L.J., Rosenberg, T., Dodge, R., Ragsdale, D.: Exploring a national cyber-security exercise for universities. IEEE Secur. Priv. **3**(5), 27–33 (2005). https://doi.org/10.1109/MSP.2005.120
8. Leban, B., Bendre, M., Tabriz, P.: Web application exploits and defenses (2017). https://google-gruyere.appspot.com/
9. Linde, R.R.: Operating system penetration. In: Proceedings of the AFIPS 1975 National Computer Conference, pp. 361–268. ACM, New York, May 1975. https://doi.org/10.1145/1499949.1500018
10. Mullins, B.E., Lacey, T.H., Mills, R.F., Trechter, J.M., Bass, S.D.: How the cyber defense exercise shaped an information-assurance curriculum. IEEE Secur. Priv. **5**(5), 40–49 (2007). https://doi.org/10.1109/MSP.2007.111
11. Pusey, P., Gondree, M., Peterson, Z.: The outcomes of cybersecurity competitions and implications for underrepresented populations. IEEE Secur. Priv. **14**(6), 90–95 (2016). https://doi.org/10.1109/MSP.2016.119

12. Pusey, P., OBrien, C.W., Lightner, L.: Preparing for the collegiate cyber defense competition (CCDC): a guide for new teams and recommendations for experienced players. National Cyberwatch Center, Largo, January 2015. https://www.nationalcyberwatch.org/resource/resource-guide-preparing-for-the-collegiate-cyber-defense-competition-ccdc-a-guide-for-new-teams-and-recommendations-for-experienced-players-2/

13. Vigna, G.: Teaching network security through live exercises. In: Irvine, C., Armstrong, H. (eds.) Security Education and Critical Infrastructures. IFIPAICT, vol. 125, pp. 3–18. Springer, Boston (2003). https://doi.org/10.1007/978-0-387-35694-5_2

14. Vigna, G., Borgolte, K., Corbetta, J., Doupe, A., Fratantonio, Y., Invernizzi, L., Kirat, D., Shoshitaishvili, Y.: Ten years of iCTF: the good, the bad, and the ugly. In: Proceedings of the 2014 USENIX Summit on Gaming, Games, and Gamification in Security Education. USENIX Association, Berkeley, August 2014. https://www.usenix.org/conference/3gse14/summit-program/presentation/vigna

15. Werther, J., Zhivich, M., Leek, T., Zeldovich, N.: Experiences in cyber security education: the MIT Lincoln laboratory capture-the-flag exercise. In: Proceedings of the Fourth Workshop on Cyber Security Experimentation and Test. USENIX Association, Berkeley, August 2011. http://static.usenix.org/legacy/events/cset11/tech/final_files/Werther.pdf

ForenCity: A Playground
for Self-Motivated Learning
in Computer Forensics

Frans F. Blauw and Wai Sze Leung(✉)

University of Johannesburg, Johannesburg, South Africa
{fblauw,wsleung}@uj.ac.za

Abstract. Striking a balance between theory and practice in computer forensics education is considered essential to producing successful graduates with the necessary skills to take on cybersecurity challenges in the workplace. Adequately incorporating both such aspects can be particularly challenging, especially in courses or modules offered within a short time-frame. In such situations, preparing the students will require that they are incentivized to actively engage with the extensive background learning material and remain current on latest developments to correctly grasp the theoretical underpinning of the subject. In this paper, we describe the development of an adventure game to make the learning of applicable theory attractive and relevant. ForenCity takes the form of a web-based scavenger hunt in which students must apply their knowledge of computer forensics and correctly process digital evidence and progress through the game.

Keywords: Game-based learning · Self-motivated learning
Computer forensics education

1 Introduction

A significant challenge that educators encounter when teaching computer forensics is being able to cover the subject matter adequately. Much debate exists on the topic of what content should go into a computer or digital forensics curriculum, with numerous research efforts dedicated to the topic [1,2]. Critics of training-based courses argue that teaching the subject as a series of steps to be followed in a laboratory produces graduates lacking the theoretical underpinning of the tasks involved [2]. Similarly, academics placing too much emphasis on theoretical knowledge may result in digital investigators sorely lacking concerning practical experience [3].

As cyberthreats grow increasingly sophisticated [4], attempts to achieve a cybsersecure society may depend on educators being able to produce professionals sufficiently skilled in identifying, collecting, preserving, and analyzing digital

L. Drevin and M. Theocharidou (Eds.): WISE 2018, IFIP AICT 531, pp. 15–27, 2018.
https://doi.org/10.1007/978-3-319-99734-6_2

artifacts [5]. Understanding how cybercriminals operate is essential for informing cybersecurity experts in their tasks [5].

As a branch of computer science, computer forensics naturally requires an understanding of computer systems, their underlying technology, and how these technologies work [2]. This "prerequisite knowledge," which not all students may necessarily possess must be met as part of the curriculum. However, in cases where the offering is limited to a short time frame, covering this knowledge may be a luxury that is ill-afforded, prompting students to acquire this knowledge elsewhere – either in other modules or by engaging in self-study. Success in computer forensics can, therefore, depend on how educators find ways to encourage their students in actively taking charge of their learning.

One potential and popular strategy is to adopt a game-based approach and deliver the content so that students learn abstract concepts and explore digital forensic processes and technologies in a much more interactive manner [6]. Such an approach represents an attractive option as the learning process allows students to overcome different challenges [7].

A second approach (not unique to computer forensics), is the adoption of blended learning [8] where the best of both physical and digital worlds are combined to deliver education services and grant students greater control over their own studying [9].

The leveraging of mobile technology in several initiatives have demonstrated that the combination of both strategies above can be quite successful. In one case, a teacher was able to take their class on a virtual tour of Africa [10] while another offered users an interactive, guided tour of the less popular points of interest on campus [11].

Inspired by such cases, we propose the development of ForenCity, a mobile adventure game in which players must draw on cross-disciplinary techniques and knowledge to investigate a case. While systems for developing mobile adventures (such as ARIS) already exist, the need to develop our own arose from two shortcomings, namely (i) the need to promote variations and encourage independent problem solving amongst students, (ii) who primarily owned Android smart devices.

This paper thus reports specifically on our process of designing and developing such a game, including the game engine. Section 2 describes specific requirements for the use of games in achieving active learning, leading to details of the design of our new game engine in Sect. 3. Section 4 details the implementation of our game system while Sect. 5 describes how a particular game offering was presented using ForenCity. Section 6 discusses plans for future implementation improvements to the system while Sect. 7 concludes the paper.

2   Designing an Effective Learning Tool

While research is careful to acknowledge that attempts to accurately quantify the efficacy of games in learning remain immature at best, the overwhelming view regards games in a favorable light, subject to a number of guidelines [12]:

- **Promote social learning and team-teaching** – permit students to work (and learn) together.
- **Feedback that is beneficial to the attainment of success** – provide appropriate hints/clues to ensure that students can progress.
- **Balance between playability and learning outcomes** – ensure that the game is equally fun to take part in while activities align with appropriate assessment opportunities.

With these requirements in mind, the following section describes the design of the ForenCity Engine that enables us to present to our Computer Forensics students with an opportunity that encourages further self-study and to apply their theoretical knowledge practically.

3   ForenCity Engine Design

ForenCity consists of two distinct modules: the ForenCity Game Client and ForenCity Maker. ForenCity Maker is the administrative side of the ForenCity Engine to build and manage a ForenCity-based game. The player will interact with the ForenCity Game Client. A basic interface provides the player with feedback as they progress through their adventure.

3.1   Design Influence

First released in May 1984, the Adventure Game Interpreter (AGI) was a high-level game engine built by Sierra On-Line to build adventure games for series such as King's Quest, Police Quest, Space Quest, and Leisure Suit Larry [13].

Following in 1987, LucasArts developed the Script Creation Utility for Maniac Mansion (SCUMM) to ease the development of Maniac Mansion, and later the first of the Monkey Island series [14].

In 1997, Chris Jones released Adventure Game Studio (AGS) that "provides the tools to make your own adventure, for free!"[15].

All these engines (AGI, SCUMM, and AGS) use locations, characters, items, dialogue, and a basic custom scripting as building blocks to create an adventure.

For the ForenCity Engine, we took the idea of building blocks to create our adventures. Each adventure is broken up into several scenes, each with their description and requirements to complete. Individual players traverse from scene to scene to complete their adventure.

3.2   Basic Gameplay Activity

First, a game creator must create several scenes using the ForenCity Maker. Each scene will contain a basic description as well as requirements that players must meet to progress to the following scene. Only players registered on the system will be able to participate in the game. Section 4.1 discusses the ForenCity Maker in greater detail.

The player can now load the ForenCity Game Client by entering the ForenCity URL for the specific adventure. They will be presented with a login page where they can log in with credentials provided to them. Once logged in, the ForenCity Engine will see at which scene the player currently is and load the appropriate scene description.

Based on the scene description, the player can be presented with scene information, describing their whereabouts and progress. If a file is available to be downloaded, the player has access to a "Download" link. Likewise, if a YouTube video is available, the video will be loaded.

The player now has the option to "scan" the scene. When a player scans the scene, the game engine will determine their current location (based on their GPS coordinates). If the location matches the required location as set up by the creator, the engine will display a success message. Otherwise, a "nothing found" message is displayed.

If a follow-up question is required after completing a scene, the client displays the question, prompting the player to answer it. Otherwise, players will automatically progress to the following scene.

Once a player reaches the end of their adventure, they will be presented with a "success" message.

4   ForenCity Engine Implementation

ForenCity Game Engine Backend. The ForenCity Game Engine (both the Game Client and Maker) is built using PHP with a JSON datastore.

PHP is a widely-used web development scripting language. Many Linux web hosts provide PHP for dynamic websites, with such packages often available on the cheapest packages.

Relational databases (such as MySQL) often come at a premium on webhosts, and so we decided to store the engine's data in JSON (JavaScript Object Notation) files. JSON is a lightweight format (as opposed to XML) and PHP has built-in JSON parsing features. Using JSON comes at the price of not having relational data to easily produce information. However, due to the linear nature of an adventure, it was not seen as a problem.

HTML5 markup was used to render client-side pages. HTML5 includes basic layout structuring but also gave us access to the device's GPS information (this is discussed later).

ForenCity Game Client. The ForenCity Game Client is built as a mobile-first web application to allow cross compatibility among many devices. The only requirement is a modern smartphone with an HTML5 compatible web browser, camera, and GPS capabilities.

jQuery Mobile 1.4.5 was used to create the user interface for the Game Client. Even though newer technologies (such as Bootstrap) are available, we believed that jQuery Mobile gave us a more comfortable "all-in-one" package that immediately produces a web app that looks complete and familiar to a user.

ForenCity Maker. ForenCity Maker's only requirement is a modern web browser. Bootstrap 3.3.7 was used to create the user interface that renders on both desktop and mobile devices [16]. The navigation bar and menu give easy access to all modules in the Maker.

4.1 ForenCity Maker

The Maker allows a game creator to manage an adventure using three modules: Game Manager, Scene Creator, and Player Manager.

Game Manager. The Game Manager provides basic administrative functionality for the Game Engine. From this module, a game creator can enable or disable the adventure, set the adventure name, set the default GPS radius, and many more options.

Scene Creator. The Scene Creator allows the game creator to create different scenes. Each scene has a *scene description* that is composed of a set of elements such as the scene's ID, its name, the description shown to the player as well as all clue data and requirements.

Scene Variables. Scene variables allow the creator to personalise the adventure's experience for each player. For instance, names and adjectives can be personalised in the scene's description. The YouTube video and GPS coordinates requirement can also be set individually for each player. When a scene loads for a player, variables will be replaced by individual values as defined in the player description and set in the Player Manager.

Player Manager. Each player in the game has a set of elements including their login username and password, their name how they are addressed by the game as well as their unique variables.

Player Variables. For each variable that has been defined in a scene description by the creator, the actual value of the variable can be set for each player. ForenCity Maker provides a simple interface that displays all players and their respective variable definitions to allow a creator to quickly change them.

4.2 Download Implementation

Some scenes allow the user to download a file. The file can be specific to the scene or the particular player. Regardless of the file to be downloaded, the filename of the file can be set in the scene description.

Due to the stateless nature of HTTP, a download link can easily be shared between users. We overcame this by generating a unique download link for each player. The link contains a key which consisting of the player's ID and the scene for which the download is available. This key is encrypted using Aaron Francis's Urlcrypt module [17] that produces URL-friendly encrypted strings. When a player selects the download link, the Game Engine will decrypt the URL key. If it is a valid download, the file will be served to the player.

4.3   GPS Scene Requirement

An adventure relies heavily on a player's GPS coordinates. Using a browser-based web application, we made use of HTML5's geolocation component [18]. The geolocation component uses the mobile device's location services to obtain the current GPS coordinates. GPS coordinates are then loaded into form inputs and sent to the server.

Browser Requirements. Apart from having location services on the device, the user must allow the site to access their location. When first loading a site that requires geolocating, the browser will prompt the user for permission. A site requesting location information must be loaded via HTTPS. Otherwise, the browser will not even prompt the user for permission.

Obtaining GPS Coordinates. HTML5 gives two methods to request the current location of a device.

The first is "navigator.geolocation.getCurrentPosition". This method simply asks the device for its current location. The device can then provide the GPS coordinates. However, GPS modules are normally not always running on mobile devices (in order to save power). As such, a once-off location request could potentially be quite inaccurate.

The second available method is "navigator.geolocation.watchPosition". The device is now continually polled for GPS coordinates. As the GPS modules are actively running, the accuracy will be improved over a brief period. This does use more battery power, but the requests are only fulfilled if the site is currently active.

During development, we initially made use of the first method in order to save power, but found that the accuracy was out far too often, and then opted for the second method.

Using GPS Coordinates. Using simple JavaScript, the GPS coordinates are loaded into two hidden form fields (latitude and longitude). This location is then submitted along with the form to the server.

The ForenCity Game Engine now received the player's current location according to their mobile device. If the requirement for the player's current scene is a GPS location, the Game Engine will determine if the player's location matches the location requirement. However, this check is not as simple as seeing if the GPS coordinates of the player directly match the GPS coordinates of the scene requirement.

GPS coordinates on consumer devices can often be off by several meters (especially if attempted indoors). The Game Engine compensates for this by first calculating the distance between the player's submitted coordinates and the scene's requirement coordinates. If this distance is within a preset maximum radius, the game engine will accept the GPS coordinates. This maximum distance can be set on an adventure-wide level, but can also be overridden on a per-scene basis. This way, indoor scenes can have a more relaxed distance than outdoor scenes as GPS coordinates might be more inaccurate under roof or concrete.

A scene using GPS coordinates is shown as part of the ForenCity Requirements checking in Fig. 1.

4.4 QR Code Scene Requirement

Some scenes need more than GPS coordinates, such as requiring the user to scan a QR code. In these cases, the player will not be presented with the option to "Scan for Clues". The scene description should give an indication that something more is required to complete the scene. QR codes can merely contain more information for the player to progress or can be used as proof that a player observed (and handled) a physical item in the real world.

Once a player scans a ForenCity QR code, the ForenCity Engine will first determine if a valid player is logged in. If not, the player will be presented with the login screen.

Since some scenes may require GPS coordinates in addition to a QR code being scanned, the player will be presented with the option to "examine" this new clue once the scene has been loaded. This allows the client to submit GPS coordinates to the server as well.

If the QR code is valid for the player's current scene, the Game Engine will perform a GPS check and allow the player to progress. If the QR code is not valid for the scene, the player will be presented with a normal "nothing found" description.

QR Code Generation. The ForenCity Maker provides a QR Code generator that generates a standard URL encoded QR Code. The URL consists of the current adventure's base URL as well as a key consisting of the scene's ID in an encrypted form, once again encrypted using Urlcrypt.

4.5 Miscellaneous Functionality

Logging. As ForenCity is first and foremost an implementation for a computer forensics game, it would obviously require that all actions performed by the player are logged. Such information enables us to monitor how each student progresses through the game to unlock the next part of the game. To achieve this, a log file is created that shows exactly what they are attempting. Each log entry includes the current date and time, the player's current IP address, the player's current GPS coordinates and the action that was performed:

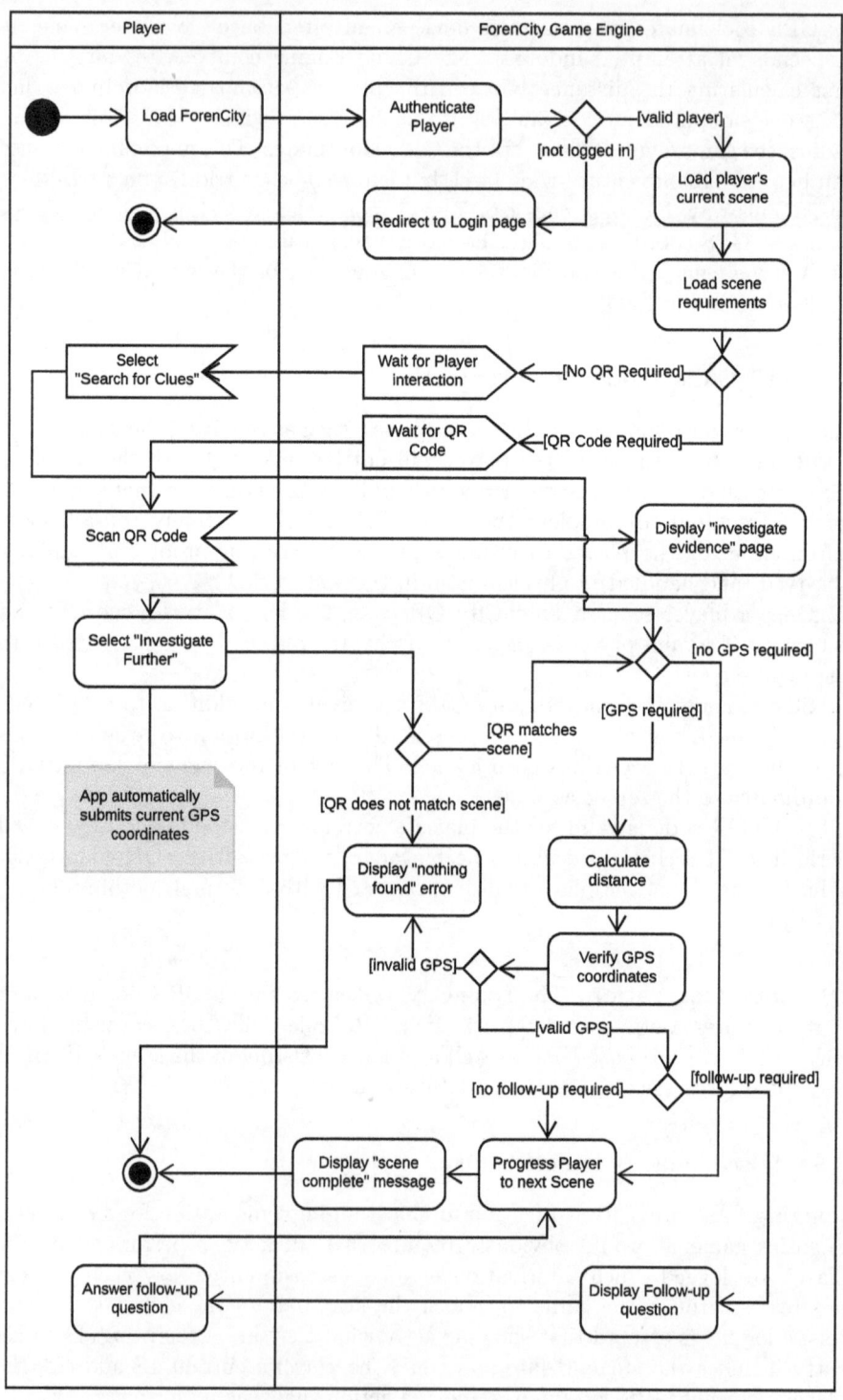

Fig. 1. ForenCity Requirement checking

- Player logs in and out.
- Player loads a scene.
- Player downloads a file.
- Player reaches a GPS or QR goal and progresses.
- Player is presented with and answers a follow-up question.
- Player attempts but fails, to progress to the next scene.
- Cheat attempt.

Anti-Cheating. Several anti-cheat features have been implemented. All cheat attempts are also logged.

- **Session Hijacking** – A player attempting to hijack another player's authenticated session will have their session automatically destroyed. This can happen if a player shares their cookie with another player. The ForenCity Engine captures the IP Address and User Agent of the player when they log in and then compares it with every page load. If either does not match, the session is destroyed.
- **Download Link Sharing** – Every download link is unique to the player (this enables each player to work with evidence files containing variations unique to that player). If the player shares the link with a fellow player, the ForenCity Engine will not allow the file to be downloaded.
- **Follow-up Question Hijacking** – A player could share the form where the follow-up question is asked with a fellow player, in order to potentially bypass an actual GPS or QR code check. Every Follow-up Question form has a unique key for every player. If the key is not present for the correct player, the answer will be rejected.

Having described the various features of ForenCity, the following section will now describe a particular case set up for a group of students.

5 Solving for a Kidnapping

In 2017, we "deputized" 15 students as investigators, tasking them to investigate the kidnapping of a mining magnate's young daughter. The case is, in essence, a race against time (although students were given the space of a week to conclude drafting a final report on how they reached the end goal).

This section showcases select scenes from the game, detailing the activities taking place, and expected outcomes from the students.

- **Scene 1: Police Headquarters (Debriefing)**
    - **Description:** Investigators view a video in which Detective Sergeant Tango debriefs them on their latest case: the kidnapping of Gugu, the daughter of a mining magnate. The only clue available at present is an email that the perpetrator(s) sent to Gugu's father from a disposable temporary email address. Attached is a photograph of Gugu along with the demand for 888 Bitcoin, to be credited into a Bitcoin wallet.

- **Expectations:** The student must analyze the email for clues. The student should notice (in their final report) that the email is from a throwaway address. The attached photograph, however, contains metadata that includes coordinates suggesting Gugu's last known location (when the photograph was taken). If the student is not familiar with how GPS coordinates work, they will now need to research how to decipher the values to visit the location physically.
- Scene 2: Gotham Heights (The First Witness)
    - **Description:** Investigators arriving at the location of the coordinates will be greeted by a cranky caretaker who complains about a "suspicious individual with a crying kid." Being very alert, he not only gives the investigator a description of the van that the suspect drives (the name of a business is given), but also provides a USB that the suspicious individual had dropped in a hurry.
    - **Expectations:** To "receive" the USB, the student downloads a file of the image. A cursory scan of the USB reveals a single file, the same photograph of Gugu attached in the ransom email. However, by making use of appropriate forensic tools, the student will recover a deleted file: a password-protected PDF. Students may attempt to crack the password with appropriate tools. However, it is expected that the student should rather pursue the other clue about the van as the business refers to a popularly known business that can be physically found on the university campus.
- *«Scenes 3 and 4 cut for brevity»*
- Scene 5: The Bulgarian Consultant
    - **Description:** The investigator makes their way up the building, arriving at the fourth floor where they are greeted by the Bulgarian Information Broker who is rumored to have many connections and holds the right answers. She gestures towards a code on her office window before returning to her work.
    - **Expectations:** Being in a building where it will be difficult to ascertain the student's position in terms of floor level, a QR code is provided as the next clue. We had previously made arrangements with our faculty's librarian to play the role of the "Bulgarian Information Broker". The student scans this QR code to obtain another set of coordinates that will lead them to an Internet café.
- *«Scenes 6 and 7 cut for brevity»*
- Scene 8: The Locker
    - **Description:** After questioning the witness in the previous scene, the investigator approaches the locker where the suspect is believed to have been loitering about previously. Some answers have been uncovered but there may be further clues that could cement the case for the investigator. Unfortunately, the locker is secured with a padlock and they are only in possession of the first three digits of the four-digit combination. It is also now, that Detective Sergeant Tango calls, ordering the investigator to finalize their investigator and put together a report.

- **Expectations:** The student may attempt to open the locker in one of two ways: since only one digit is missing, it is possible to apply brute force and test out all ten possible combinations. Alternatively, a physical clue in the previous step may yield indented writing of the combination written on a notepad. The game is set such that a variety of choices made throughout the game may yield the same end result. However, the majority of marks awarded will come from the student's ability to correctly motivate their rationale for carrying out a certain action, as detailed in their final report.

6   Future Implementation

Following with our influences (Sect. 3.1), we want ForenCity Engine to have more than only scenes. As indicated in Sect. 2, we plan to create a more non-linear adventure where players will have the opportunity to explore all scenes at any time and interact with characters, interactive objects, and an inventory system.

- **Non-Linear Gameplay** – the current ForenCity Game Engine only allows for a linear story to be told. However, in real-life, different investigators' reasoning might lead them to different clues first. As such, we want most scenes to be available from the start of the adventure, but giving (or removing) information as different tasks are completed. Different scenes might also change depending on the time of day.
- **Characters** – Forensic investigation is not only limited to inanimate objects. Often interaction (and interrogation) with other people will be required. We want to develop a character component that will include a complete dialogue tree system. Players will have the opportunity to meet with these virtual characters and have interactions with them. Depending on their dialogue choices, characters will either reveal or withhold vital information.
- **Interactive Objects** – Forensic investigate will require interaction with objects at a scene. Similar to Characters described above, we want to implement a component where the player can interact with virtual objects to reveal more information. Interactions can be limited to something simple such as switching a "light" on or off. More complicated interactions can include performing a search and finding files on a computer.
- **Inventory** – Often one piece of evidence will lead to more and different clues. As the player progresses through their adventure, they should be able to pick up items along the way. Items can then be used alongside other items, objects or even characters.

7   Conclusion

As seen in our discussion on the various features of ForenCity, we have developed a platform that enables educators to create engaging and customized problem-based assessments in the form of an adventure game that takes students beyond the physical classroom. Based on participants' feedback, we enjoyed a rather positive and enthusiastic response from students excited to draw on their computer science and computer forensics knowledge in order to unlock the next clue and reveal how the next chapter in the mystery would unfold.

In ForenCity, we were able to create an environment that augmented physical items and spaces on our institution's campus with virtual characters and props to guide each student through a police investigation that developed as they engaged with both the physical and virtual props around them. Restricted only by our imagination and storytelling skills, ForenCity could potentially be used to assess students on a variety of other cybersecurity skills. Beyond implementing the extra features in ForenCity, we look forward to expanding ForenCity's storyline, inviting students in other subjects to test their mettle while getting to apply and experience the skills and knowledge they have acquired thus far.

References

1. Irons, A.D., Stephens, P., Ferguson, R.I.: Digital Investigation as a distinct discipline: a pedagogic perspective. Digital Invest. **6**, 82–90 (2009)
2. Lang, A., Bashir, M., Campbell, R., Destefano, L.: Developing a new digital forensics curriculum. Digital Invest. **11**, S76–S84 (2014)
3. Willems, C., Meinel, C.: Online assessment for hands-on cyber security training in a virtual lab. In: Proceedings of the 2012 IEEE Global Engineering Education Conference (EDUCON), pp. 1–10. IEEE, Princeton (2012)
4. Six Cyber Threats to Really Worry About in 2018. https://www.technologyreview.com/s/609641/six-cyber-threats-to-really-worry-about-in-2018/
5. Cyber Security Awareness Month: Cyber Security vs. Cyber Forensics. http://www.stevenson.edu/online/blog-news-events/cyber-security-vs-cyber-forensics
6. Pan, Y., Schwartz, D., Mishra, S.: Gamified digital forensics course modules for undergraduates. In: 2015 IEEE Integrated STEM Education Conference, pp. 100–105. IEEE, Princeton (2015)
7. What is Game-based learning? https://www.game-learn.com/what-is-game-based-learning/
8. Blended learning is the future. https://mg.co.za/article/2017-03-17-00-blended-learning-is-the-future
9. Graham, C.R.: Blended learning systems: definition, current trends, and future directions. In: Handbook of Blended Learning: Global Perspectives, Local Designs, pp. 3–21. Pfeiffer Publishing, San Francisco (2006)
10. ARIS: A Field Day Lab Experiment. https://fielddaylab.org/make/aris/
11. Garay-Cortes, J., Uribe-Quevedo, A.: Location-based augmented reality game to engage students in discovering institutional landmarks. In: 2016 7th International Conference on Information, Intelligence, Systems Applications (IISA), pp. 1–4. IEEE, Princeton (2016)
12. de Freitas, S.: Are games effective learning tools? a review of educational games. Educ. Technol. Soc. **21**(2), 74–84 (2018)
13. Adventure Game Interpreter. https://en.wikipedia.org/wiki/Adventure_Game_Interpreter
14. Script Creation Utility for Maniac Mansion (SCUMM). https://en.wikipedia.org/wiki/SCUMM
15. Adventure Game Studio. http://www.adventuregamestudio.co.uk/

16. Bootstrap. https://getbootstrap.com/
17. Urlcrypt. https://github.com/cheerful/URLcrypt
18. HTML5 Geolocation. https://www.w3schools.com/Html/html5_geolocation.asp

Developing Hands-On Laboratory Works for the "Information Security Incident Management" Discipline

Natalia Miloslavskaya$^{(\boxtimes)}$ and Alexander Tolstoy

The National Research Nuclear University
MEPhI (Moscow Engineering Physics Institute),
31 Kashirskoye shosse, Moscow, Russia
{NGMiloslavskaya, AITolstoj}@mephi.ru

Abstract. The paper presents our recent experience in developing the hands-on laboratory works for the "Business Continuity and Information Security Maintenance" Master's Degree programme in the framework of the NRNU MEPhI's "Network Security Intelligence" Educational and Research Center (NSIC). These labs are designed for the "Information Security Incident Management" discipline to provide training on information security (IS) incident practical and actionable response, in particular its investigation on the basis of computer forensic approaches and specialized tools being used for these purposes. The main areas of further improvement of these labs conclude the paper.

Keywords: Information security incident · Online banking services
Money transfer · Hands-on laboratory work · Computer forensics

1 Introduction

In the face of ever-increasing Information Security (IS) incidents, many standards determine the need for organizations to timely identify and respond to them [1]. In 2012, satisfying the urgent demand for a specific IS specialists, the "Business Continuity and Information Security Maintenance" two-years (4 semesters) Master's Degree programme was launched at the "Information Security of Banking Systems" Department of the NRNU MEPhI. The "Information Security Incident Management" discipline is included in the curriculum. Its main provisions are illustrated on the typical transferring money cases for the Online Banking Services (OBS).

Taking into account the OBS specifics, IS incident when transferring money refers to an IS event or their combination, indicating an accomplished, ongoing or probable IS threat implementation, which results in (1) the destructive impact on organizations' or clients' information infrastructure components (together called II components) used for money transfer (MT), which led/may lead to a violation of the payment service provision continuity, or (2) an unauthorized MT by persons without the right to dispose of funds that led/may lead to MT by order of persons who do not have such rights, non-temporal MT or MT using distorted payment details in the MT orders [2]. The key areas of response to these IS incidents are the following: identification of IS threat

© IFIP International Federation for Information Processing 2018
Published by Springer Nature Switzerland AG 2018. All Rights Reserved
L. Drevin and M. Theocharidou (Eds.): WISE 2018, IFIP AICT 531, pp. 28–39, 2018.
https://doi.org/10.1007/978-3-319-99734-6_3

implementation methods and schemes based on the collection and analysis of technical data (TDs) generated by II components (including Information Protection Tools, IPTs), used by organizations and clients for MT; prevention of repeated IS incidents based on previously used methods and schemes; identification of IS threats' sources, based on TDs processing results; and conducting timely detection of markers for "hidden" unauthorized II components' management (known as Indicators of Compromise, IoCs) based on TDs processing results. To ensure that these activities can be performed within the IS incident management system (including collection and recording of information about the IS incident), organizations should apply methods of collecting, processing, analyzing and documenting the TDs. At the same time, the TDs collection and further extracting the content (semantic information) from them should be conducted by persons having the necessary experience and competence.

All teachers are aware that a theory is not viable without practice, as any theory is better understood when it can be practiced. That is why to develop more enhanced students' skills in IS incident management within the greater opportunities that appeared after creation of the "Network Security Intelligence" Educational and Research Center (NSIC) at the NRNU MEPhI [3] it was decided to update the laboratory works (labs) for the above discipline, which was previously focused on the study of Intrusion Detection and Prevention systems (IDPSs), Security Information and Event Management systems and security scanners. Thus the paper is organized as follows. Section 2 provides a brief review of related work. General description of the developed labs is given in Sect. 3. The basic principles of performing the labs are presented in Sect. 4. Section 5 is devoted to the regulatory framework used for the labs creation. Students' assignments and labs' scenario are described in detail in Sect. 6. The recommended strategies for the collected TDs analysis and investigative software are listed in Sects. 7 and 8 respectively. The laboratory testbed is discussed in Sect. 9. The main areas of further improvement of our labs conclude the paper.

2   Related Work

Computer forensics learning has begun to be dealt with for a long time and a lot has already been written on this topic by now. Let us mention only a few most interesting from our point of view publications, showing their main focus. Majority of publications from the early 2000s examined forensics education in general (like in [4]) and its possible curriculum [5]. Further works were devoted to teaching forensics to a specialized target groups like undergraduate students [6] or experts with their further certification [7–10]. In parallel, the issues of implementing common labs [11–13] and conducting some specific labs within the framework of courses offered by different training centers [9, 14–16] are discussed. For example, at present there are a lot of certifications in the area: *Vendor-Specific*: EnCase Certified Examiner (EnCE) and AccessData Certified Examiner (ACE); *Vendor-Neutral*: Certified Forensic Computer Examiner (CFCE) and Electronic Evidence Collection Specialist (CEECS) by International Association of Computer Investigative Specialists; Certified Forensic Analyst (GCFA) and Examiner (GCFE) by SANS GIAC; Computer Hacking Forensic Investigator (CHFI) by EC-Council; Certified Computer Crime Investigator (CCCI) and

Forensic Technician (CCFT) by High-Tech Crime Network, and other certifications by Computer Technology Investigators Network, High Technology Crime Investigation Association, etc.

The usage of open source tools while teaching computer forensics is also long and widely popularized [17, 18].

As we have so far developed only one, but useful for the purpose of IS incident management lab, we do not want to be compared and compete with all these recognized leaders in computer forensics training and certification; we just want to learn their best practices.

3   General Description of the Labs Developed

The "Information Security Incident Management" discipline (3 credits) is one of the core courses of the above Master's Degree programme, and computer forensics and investigation is not its main specialization. It is obvious and does not require long explanations that "Incident Response" is more general concept than "Computer Forensics" originated in the late 1980s (of course, with this wording, we do not want to underestimate its importance). At a minimum, incident response involves also pre-incident preparations, all necessary organizational activities around the computer forensics process and post-incident actions with lessons learnt. In turn, computer forensics process is initiated after an incident is detected for its actual investigation.

The discipline is taught at the 3rd semester (after the "Information Security Risk Management" discipline and in parallel with the "Information Technology Security Assessment" discipline) and consists of 16 h of lectures, 16 h of labs and 36 h of various forms of student's independent work under instructor's supervision.

The discipline goal is to study the methods and tools of IS incident management (with cases for the banking organizations of the Russian Federation), as well as the main approaches to the development, implementation, operation, analysis, maintenance and improvement of IS incident management systems (ISIMSs) of a particular organization to be protected. One of the sections of the discipline is devoted to the IS incident response teams (ISIRTs). Among other things, the ISIRT's work with the IS incident's digital evidence should be given special attention. Hence, we developed our hands-on labs keeping in mind their target audience – future ISIRT's experts.

As it is approved in the discipline's syllabus and following the requirements of the Bank of Russia Standard STO BR IBBS-1.3-2016 [2], after these labs our students will obtain the following basic skills and abilities (learning outcomes), namely:

- To organize IS incident management, in particular the collection and analysis of IS incident information to decide on a subsequent response;
- To participate in the design and operation of the organization's ISIMSs, in particular in the activities of ISIRTs;
- To develop drafts of organizational and administrative documents, as well as technical and operational documentation for ISIMSs and make a choice and use tools for managing IS incidents.

4   Basic Principles of Performing the Labs

On the labs, the activity of ISIRT's members is simulated when collecting the TDs from the II components involved in MT and searching for and extracting the content (semantic information) from the collected TDs for further deep analysis. Doing this, students should learn to observe the following important principles of their behavior. All downloads and installations during labs must be coordinated with the instructor. Any procedures and service commands performed for TDs processing should not make changes to the original TDs and/or their reference copies. The implementation of all procedures and service commands for TDs processing should be accompanied by the implementation of procedures and service commands that should provide their availability and confidentiality, as well as the opportunity to monitor their integrity (invariability). TDs processing should be accompanied by the description and logging, among other things, of all procedures and service commands performed, as well as a list of the technical tools used. When collecting the TDs, any means/materials that produce/emit a static or electromagnetic field should be avoided, as it can damage/destroy the collected TDs. Less powerful PCs should be used for routine tasks and multipurpose PCs for high-end analysis. This list can be expanded if necessary.

5   Regulatory Framework for the Labs

When developing the labs we followed all the recommendations of the following regulations (excluded from the References deliberately not to make them very large and not cited on every page again and again as the basis for all our conclusions):

1. International: Standards by ISO/IEC: 27035:2016 Information technology – Security techniques – Information security incident management – Part 1: Principles of incident management and Part 2: Guidelines to plan and prepare for incident response; 27037:2012 Guidelines for identification, collection and/or acquisition and preservation of digital evidence; 27041:2015 Guidance on assuring suitability and adequacy of incident investigative method; 27042:2015 Guidelines for the analysis and interpretation of digital evidence; 27043:2015 Incident investigation principles and processes; 30121:2015 IT – Governance of digital forensic risk framework; Special Publications (SP) by NIST: 800–61r2 Computer Security Incident Handling Guide; 800-86 Guide to Integrating Forensic Techniques into Incident Response; 800-92 Guide to Computer Security Log Management; 800-101r1 Guidelines on Mobile Device Forensics; Publications by the SANS Institute, the European Network of Forensic Science Institutes, the Scientific Working Group on Digital Evidence; etc.;
2. National: Bank of Russia Recommendations on Standardization RS BR IBBS-2.5-2014 «Maintenance of Information Security of the Russian Banking System Organizations. Management of Information Security Incidents» and Standard STO BR IBBS-1.3-2016 «....Collection and Analysis of Technical Data When Responding to Information Security Incidents during Money Transfer» [2].

6   Students' Assignments and Labs' Scenario

The objective of these hands-on labs is to provide our students an expert knowledge about the tools used in computer forensics for gathering digital evidence, viewing files of various formats, locating files needed for investigation, performing image and file conversions, handling evidence data, creating a disk image file of a hard disk partition, recovering deleted files from a hard disk, etc., as well as to gain practical skills in locating and examining evidence on devices and forensic images, analyzing and reporting findings. For that purpose the labs follow a cohesive scenario simulating a real IS incident investigation.

Based on the goals and complexity of tasks performed during the labs, the time required to complete the labs assignment is 4 h (2 times 2 h each in 2 different days). From our point of view it is sufficient to obtain the appropriate basic skills and abilities listed above. The work is divided into two days deliberately in order to teach the students to retain digital evidence in case they cannot be collected at one time.

At the time of labs one group of Masters is divided into a few subgroups (4 students in each subgroup), who are assigned to investigate different categories of IS incidents. When performing the labs, the students get assignments related to 6 categories of IS events when transferring money (leading to the specific IS incident types):

1. Identification and authentication of OBS administrators, customers and processes;
2. Access control to all II components used by OBS front-/back-office and clients;
3. Remote access to the II components;
4. Changing the state of the II components;
5. Anti-virus protection;
6. IPTs' functioning.

During a week before labs devoted to investigation of one predefined category of IS events the students of the same group, but from other subgroups (not assigned to study it), are invited to the laboratory at any working time to implement this event and create a lot of traffic and emulate a variety of suspicious activities. Before any actions taken, they should inform their instructor on what they are going to do and what specific tools they are going to use for that purpose and get his consent to this. Thus, everything that happens in the laboratory is under the constant supervision of the instructor and will not harm other users of the laboratory.

As a part of the labs, the students must collect and document the TDs for each detected IS incident of a specific type, which was given them by their instructor, and overview information about it (so called IS incident profile) describing the way they used to identify the IS incident; the source of information about the IS incident; the content of information about the IS incident received from the source; the scenario for the implementation of the IS incident; the date and time of IS incident detection; the II components involved in the implementation of the IS incident, as well as suffered from it, including the level of the IS incident severity for the object being selected by the students for labs; the ways to connect the II components involved in the implementation of the IS incident to the Internet (including information about an Internet service provider) or another University subnetworks, etc.

Before the TDs collection, the students must describe and fix by a camera (with a correct date and time stamp and information about its manufacturer, model and serial number) the TDs collection site, including the following: type, location, power state of the II components; availability and way of their connecting to networks, including wireless networks and the Internet; and information about events and processes on the II components displays (if applicable).

Based on our deep analysis of a huge number of different typical network attacks' scenarios that we conduct since 1995 and our 22-years experience of teaching network security at the NRNU MEPhI (one short note: our first textbook entitled "Vulnerabilities and Protection Methods in the Global Internet" was published in Russian in 1997), we work out our own IoCs for wide-spread IS incidents when transferring money using OBS. Further, we will no longer refer to our experience and long-term studies, but we will imply that the results presented are based on them.

Thus, the students must collect, analyze and document the following TDs containing these IoCs, specific for the event category assigned to them:

- Nonvolatile TDs located on the II components' memories (including those used to maintain the functioning and administration of the network, not just OBS);
- Volatile TDs located in the RAM of the II components and volatile TDs of the II components' operating systems (OS): data on network configurations and connections, running software processes, open files; list of open access sessions; system date and time;
- Logs of database management systems (DBMS); network equipment used in the network: routers, switches, wireless access points and controllers, modems; tools used to provide remote access (VPN gateways); DHCP services; IPTs used on the II components: authentication, authorization and access control tools; IPTs against unauthorized access; firewalls; IDPSs; antiviruses; cryptographic IPTs;
- Logs and data of mail servers and e-mail content filtering tools as well as web-servers and web protocols content filtering tools;
- Network traffic data (its copy and/or headers) from/to a network segment, in which the II components are located and so on.

To collect the TDs, the following scenario of the students' actions was developed:

- Disconnecting the II components (their network cable) from the network and/or turning off the network devices (including Wi-Fi/Bluetooth adapter, etc.);
- Forensic copying of volatile TDs from the II components, including copying the contents of RAM and copying OS data;
- Disconnecting the II components by interrupting the power supply (disconnecting the power cord or removing the battery), disconnecting the network cable (for the use of network interfaces supporting power over the computer network, for example, Power over Ethernet), and then removing the memory devices;
- Copying of IPTs' logs and network traffic;
- Forensic copying (creation of images) of nonvolatile TDs of the II components' memory devices by bit copying and/or "bit-copy plus" copying, including copying (creating images) of hard magnetic disks of the II components.

The detailed recommendations for the students were worked out and are given to them in advance to provide the opportunity to be better prepared to work and demonstrate their knowledge on the progress test after it. For example, the specific recommendations for copying the logs, in most cases stored as data files, are the following:

1. The choice of storage media and repositories for collecting the logs of sufficient capacity, that allows to avoid the rewriting and/or loss of information significant for the purpose of responding to IS incidents;
2. Connection to the monitored object via the console port (performing remote connection via Telnet or SSH protocols is not recommended), and it is strictly recommended not to change its current configuration by entering any commands;
3. Uploading (copying) of logs for a certain required period of time in data files;
4. Calculation and saving of checksums or hashes for the copied data files;
5. Logical copying to external media (compact disks) of the source data files created at step 1;
6. Calculation and saving of checksums or hashes of the source data files created at step 1, and collection of data files copied ay step 3, comparing the calculated values with the values calculated at step 2, to confirm the integrity of the copied data with the written fixing of the results of this comparison;
7. Ensuring the adoption of all necessary measures to restrict access to collected data copies and the safe packaging and storage of information carriers containing them.

In order to complete the labs successfully, students of one subgroup must demonstrate their joint report with the results obtained, indicate each student's contribution and pass quizzes. All this forms an assessment of each student separately.

After the labs completion, the computers should be restored to their original condition by the same subgroup of students, whom prepared it for investigation before.

7   Recommended Strategies for TDs's Analysis

To conduct an in-depth analysis of the collected TDs, the students are recommended the following general strategies as well as scripting experience (Python, Perl, Ruby, etc.), which will help them to automate the analysis and reporting of results from the tasks performed.

The analysis strategy in a certain time range, which can be used if there is information about the date and time of the initial (base) IS event or their group, and includes two methods: (1) Analysis of the content information about the attributes of data files to determine the composition of data files and the subsequent analysis of the contents of data files created and/or modified for the time range associated with the IS incident; and (2) analysis of the composition and content of the logs for the time range associated with the IS incident.

The analysis strategy of deliberately hidden data, which provides the following: conducting comparative analysis and discrepancies in the content of the headers of data files (file header), data file extensions and structures; analysis of the structure and content of encrypted data files, data files protected by passwords (including archives) and data files, the contents of which are generated using steganography; analysis of information from hidden areas of hard disk drives (host-protected area, HPA); analysis of objects embedded in data files (for example, in document files); and analysis of the possible data file allocation in non-standard places in the file system.

The strategy of comparative (correlation) analysis of data files and applications, which provides the following: comparison of the composition of data files with installed applications; comparative analysis of the composition and integrity of executable data files based on the calculation of hashes and reference values; analysis of possible relations between data files and/or applications, for example, correlation of data logs of using the Internet with cache files, and data files with files contained in the attachment of e-mail messages; and identification of unknown types of data files.

For each IS incident type studied during labs, special recommendations have been developed for the students concerning the content (semantic information) that should be given special attention in the analysis. Thus, when analyzing the destructive impact of computer viruses on the II components for OBS, the students are encouraged to pay special attention to the following:

- The date and time when computer viruses appeared on the II components;
- Detection of computer viruses by antivirus, their classification by the antivirus manufacturer and the initial location of the detected components of computer viruses on the II components;
- The presence of infected files in the antiviral "quarantine" for the date range;
- The presence of extraneous software processes similar to system processes, but launched either from an uncommon place (temporary folders, folders of roaming profiles), or software processes that have a similar name to system ones;
- The presence of files and folders similar to system files and folders, but located in a different place than the standard location in the file system (for example, the Windows Update folder in the root of the Windows folder);
- The presence of uncharacteristic software launching at the II component's OS startup in startup folders, services, system drivers, the Windows registry, the task scheduler and other specific places defined by the OS type;
- The presence of a small volume of constant and/or periodic outgoing/incoming network traffic to network addresses outside/in Russia, not belonging to the list of IP addresses being maintained for an authorized data exchange;
- The presence of devices' connection data in OS's or specialized software logs;
- Atypical network traffic routes; non-typical routing tables for network devices;
- The presence of incoming messages in e-mail server logs from e-mail addresses that have a similar spelling to the government agencies' domains, or from domains, correspondence with which is not characteristic for the organization; etc.

8   Investigative Software

The STO BR IBBS-1.3-2016 [3], adopted and put into effect since 2017, was taken as the basis of the software list, from which the students is recommended to make their choice. This list contains some of the most common and well-proven tools like

Forensic Toolkit (FTK) from AccessData and it can be extended by EnCase from Guidance Software, Forensic Recovery of Evidence Device (FRED) from Digital Intelligence, the Velocity series from Tritech Forensics. These tools are available in many configurations and range in price (3,000–16,000 $ and above). We give some names of a specific open-source and commercial tools being a base for performing the tasks by the students. They should use them or if they are paid they should find their freeware analogues available on the Internet (of course, the success of this Task 0 is also evaluated by the instructor). Thus, the list below will be constantly expanded and updated.

Task 1. Perform a forensic copy (create an image) of the II components' memory devices using the following software tools or their free analogues for:

- A forensic copy: for Linux (L): dd (stands for Data Duplicator) and dc3dd; for Windows (W): FTK Imager, The Sleuth Kit, EnCase Forensic Imager and Redline; W+L: Belkasoft Evidence Center;
- Calculating hashes: L: md5sum and sha256sum; W: Memoryze; W+L: dff;
- "Write-blocker"/"Forensic bridge": W+L: Raptor; dff.

Task 2. Copy the contents of the RAM of the II components and collecting the OS data using the following software tools or their free analogues for:

- Copying the RAM content: W: FTK Imager, Redline, MoonSols Windows Memory Toolkit and Memoryze; W+L: dff and Belkasoft Evidence Center;
- Collecting the OS data on network configurations: L: ifconfig and arp; W: ipconfig, netstat, arp, route and Sysinternals; W+L: Rekall Memory Forensic Framework and Volatility Framework;
- Collecting the OS data on (1) network connections: W: nbstat, net and Sysinternals; W+L: netstat, Rekall Memory Forensic Framework and Volatility Framework; (2) running processes: W: Task Manager, Memoryze and Sysinternals; L: ps, top and w; W+L: dff, Rekall Memory Forensic Framework and Volatility Framework; (3) open files: W: Sysinternals; L: lsof; W+L: Rekall Memory Forensic Framework and Volatility Framework; (4) open access sessions: W: netstat and Sysinternals; L: w; W+L: Rekall Memory Forensic Framework and Volatility Framework;
- Collecting data on registered users, the time of their last authentication: W: net and Sysinternals; L: last, lastlog, who and w;
- Collecting the OS system date and time: W: date, time, nlsinfo and Sysinternals; L: date; W+L: Rekall Memory Forensic Framework and Volatility Framework.

Task 3. Collect data about the attributes and structure of OS files using the following software tools or their free analogues:

- L: file; W+L: dff, Belkasoft Evidence Center and The Sleuth Kit;
- For analysis of files: executable: packerid, pescanner, exescan, PEiD, PeStudio, CFF Explorer; PDF: PeePDF, PDFiD, AnalyzePDF, pdfextract, pdfwalker, pyew, pdf-parser, pdf.py, pdfsh, Malzilla; MS Office: OfficeMalScanner, Offvis, peOLEScanner; graphic: Photo Investigator, Adroit Photo Forensics, Exiftool.

Task 4. Analyze logs for registering web servers and proxy servers using the Log Analysis Tool Kit (LATK).

Task 5. Copy and analyze network traffic using the following software tools: packet sniffers like tcpdump and Wireshark (W+L); W+L: ntop; L: Network Miner, Foremost and Kismet; ssldump (for SSL/TLS traffic); DINO (for visualization of network connections and IP address geolocation).

Task 6. Analyze anomalous/malicious actions of files using Cockoo Sandbox.

Task 7. Analyze the Cisco network equipment used in the laboratory: show (with keys clock detail, version, running-config, users, who, log, debug, processes, ip route, ip ospf, ip bgp, ip arp, interfaces, ip sockets, tcp brief all, ip nat translations, snmp...).

Task 8. Analyze mobile devices in the laboratory: Belkasoft Evidence Center (demo is available),.XRY for iOS, Android, Windows Phone, Blackberry.

Task 9. Identify the owner of an IP/DNS address: web service who is; traceroute for Linux and tracert for Windows; ip source-track for Cisco routers.

Task 10. Analyze the collected TDs using the following software tools or their free analogues: REMnux, PALADIN Forensic Suite, which contain a number of software tools specified above that allow analysis of malicious and suspicious files, creation of forensic copies of RAM, memory devices and network traffic.

9   The Laboratory Testbed

The idea of giving our students an opportunity to gain practical experience in collecting and analyzing the TDs for further response to IS incident when transferring money using OBS by the way of hands-on labs lies in building and maintaining a suitable for training labs' environment. It is a daunting undertaking due to the many considerations that must be made to include room requirements, software, hardware, peripherals, devices, network topography and many other things. Our testbed is able to effectively facilitate student learning, meeting the following main requirements:

- Profitability, as the cost of forensic tools used in the laboratory should be significantly less (or even free of charge) than their cost for the real networks;
- Flexibility, as its structure should be easily reconfigurable: different labs' tasks require specific network topologies and host configurations (that is why we decided not to draw any schemes as it is one of the first tasks for the students to conduct mapping of the network under investigation);
- Scalability, for investigating all 6 categories of IS events. During one lab only one assignment to investigate only one category of IS events is fulfilled by 4 students from the main subgroup. The remaining students observe the process and can give their advice when the instructor permits;
- Reliability, as the laboratory should be able to easily recover from permitted for investigation damage by the students, as well as be able to quickly restore the default settings and network configurations for another subsequent use;
- Isolation, as the internal testbed should be isolated from the remaining part of the NSIC and not affect its operation. Each student works within the same testbed and his work should not cause any inconvenience to other NSIC users.

We deliberately do not draw the testbed's diagram here, because it will be different for six different investigations. But for all investigations its hardware includes 16 PCs on the basis of Intel Core i3 with 4 GB RAM, 500 GB of HDD, Gigabyte graphic card and DVD-ROM drives (we are going to upgrade them in 2018), and one lightweight mobile forensic workstation using a laptop PC (Lenovo ThinkPad T450 s) with USB 2.0/3.0 ports and Wireless Network Interface Card.

As for the software: 16 PCs and the laptop have access to Windows and Linux installations either as a virtual machine or on the PC directly. PDF reader, MS Office, special viewers, a decompression tool that can handle a wide variety of formats (tar, gzip, bzip, RAR, etc.) and all typical software are installed on all computers. For the educational purposes a few licenses for the OBS system were provided by our partners, but they asked not to disclose its name. In general, depending on the monetary constraints, the PCs in the testbed can be outfitted with different software solutions that range from commercial investigative suites to free command line tools. In much the same way, the forensic PCs that will be running the software can be vendor supplied standalone units or can be built with individual components in house [12].

10   Conclusion

The relevance of specialized computer forensic labs for the "Information Security Incident Management" course was determined by the urgent needs to develop more enhanced students' practical skills within the NRNU MEPhI's NSIC. We emphasize once again that we developed only one but very useful for that purposes lab with six different assignments for 6 subgroups within one student group; so it makes no sense to compare it with long-term courses of the recognized training centers specializing in forensic studies – we just learned their best practices. As for privacy, it is a separate issue that requires special study and it is out of this technically-focused paper's scope.

Our labs have two undoubted advantages: their descriptions are presented in Russian and they take into account the specifics of IS incidents for OBS as much as possible. The originality of our results is using the scenario of money transfers as a way of engaging students in a specific risk-laden activity performed globally.

One of our findings is that the successful construction and management of the testbed can be accomplished even with a small budget so long as focus remains on students' skills. The labs have been successfully tested in 2018 spring semester by two groups the 2nd year Masters during their Internship (totally 40 students). Their validation demonstrates that the proposed scenario truly works within the student groups and testbed described. All the students perform the labs with great interest.

We shared our short-term experience in designing the labs – it is a "work-in-progress" and there is still much to do. Our future work is intended to develop a unique cloud-based learning platform for investigating IS incidents and on this basis to deepen and increase the number of investigations being conducted by students.

Acknowledgement. This work was supported by the MEPhI Academic Excellence Project (agreement with the Ministry of Education and Science of the Russian Federation of August 27, 2013, project no. 02.a03.21.0005).

References

1. ISO/IEC 27000:2016 Information technology – Security techniques – Information security management systems – Overview and vocabulary
2. Bank of Russia Standard STO BR IBBS-1.3-2016 "Maintenance of Information Security of the Russian Banking System Organizations. Collection and Analysis of Technical Data When Responding to Information Security Incidents during Money Transfer"
3. Miloslavskaya, N., Tolstoy, A., Migalin, A.: "Network Security Intelligence" educational and research center. In: Bishop, M., Futcher, L., Miloslavskaya, N., Theocharidou, M. (eds.) WISE 2017. IAICT, vol. 503, pp. 157–168. Springer, Cham (2017). https://doi.org/10.1007/978-3-319-58553-6_14
4. Yasinsac, A., Erbacher, R.F., Marks, D.G., Pollitt, M.M., Sommer, P.M.: Computer forensics education. IEEE Secur. Priv. 1(4), 15–23 (2003)
5. McGuire, T.J., Murff, K.N.: Issues in the development of a digital forensics curriculum. J. Comput. Sci. Coll. 22(2), 274–280 (2006)
6. Batten, L., Pan, L.: Teaching digital forensics to undergraduate students. IEEE Secur. Priv. 6 (3), 54–56 (2008)
7. Wassenaar, D., Woo, D., Wu, P.: A certificate program in computer forensics. J. Comput. Sci. Coll. 24(4), 158–167 (2009)
8. Digital intelligence computer forensics training. https://www.digitalintelligence.com/forensictraining.php. Accessed 22 June 2018
9. InfoSec institute's authorized computer forensics boot camp. https://www.infosecinstitute.com/courses/. Accessed 22 June 2018
10. Computer and hacking forensics. https://www.cybrary.it/course/computer-hacking-forensics-analyst/. Accessed 22 June 2018
11. Scott, S.: Implementing a digital forensics lab in education. http://www.in-fosecwriters.com/Papers/SScott_Forensics_Lab_in_Education.pdf. Accessed 22 June 2018
12. Lawrence, K., Chi, H.: Framework for the design of web-based learning for digital forensics labs. In: Proceedings of the 47th Annual ACM Southeast Regional Conference, 19–21 March 2009, Clemson, SC (2009)
13. Floyd, K., Yerby, J.: Development of a digital forensics lab to support active learning. In: Southern Association for Information Systems (SAIS) 2014 Proceedings (2014)
14. DFIR Training & Courses. https://digital-forensics.sans.org/training. Accessed 22 June 2018
15. Forensic Tool Kit. http://accessdata.com/training. Accessed 22 June 2018
16. List of free online computer forensics courses and classes. https://study.com/articles/List_of_Free_Online_Computer_Forensics_Courses_and_Classes.html. Accessed 22 June 2018
17. Manson, D., Carlin, A., Ramos, S., Gyger, A., Kaufman, M., Treichelt, J.: Is the open way a better way? Digital forensics using open source tools. In: Proceedings of the 40th Annual Hawaii International Conference on System Sciences (HICSS 2007), p. 266, 3–6 January 2007, Waikoloa, Big Island, Hawaii, USA. IEEE Computer Society (2007)
18. Austin, R.D.: Digital forensics on the cheap: teaching forensics using open source tools. In: Proceedings of the 4th Annual Conference on Information Security Curriculum Development (InfoSecCD 2007), pp. 1–5, 28 September 2007, Kennesaw, Georgia. ACM (2007)

A Pilot Study in Cyber Security Education Using CyberAIMs: A Simulation-Based Experiment

Erjon Zoto[✉], Stewart Kowalski[✉], Christopher Frantz[✉], Edgar Lopez-Rojas[✉], and Basel Katt[✉]

Norwegian University of Science and Technology (NTNU), Gjøvik, Norway
{erjon.zoto,stewart.kowalski,christopher.frantz,edgar.lopez,
basel.katt}@ntnu.no

Abstract. We hardly pass any day without hearing of a new cyber attack. The recent ever-increasing occurrence of such attacks has given to researchers, practitioners and others an opportunity to raise awareness and train staff from the public and private institutions, as well as other people within the society, about the evolving nature of cyberspace threats. As a first step in this process, we aim to present main findings from a pilot study conducted with a target group of Master students with diverse backgrounds and knowledge about cyber security practices. The study was done using an agent-based simulation tool, CyberAIMs, as the core component of the experiment. Students were involved in a pre-test/post-test study in order to assess the probable change in their thinking process after using CyberAIMs. A scenario created from a real cyber case was additionally used to get the participants accustomed to the tool. The experiment is still in progress, while preliminary data indicate that there is a shift in students' perspective on the most relevant attributes affecting defense agents' performance, results that could be related to both adversarial and systems thinking processes.

Keywords: Agent-based simulation · Teaching · Cyber security
Adversarial thinking · Systems thinking · Training

1 Introduction

Cyber security events have been major headlines at an ever-increasing pace for the past recent years. Last year produced notable attacks such as WannaCry and NotPetya, while the most recent global event targeted from cyber attackers has been the Winter Olympic Games in South Korea this February.

With attacks intensifying in numbers and covering more and more unpredictable targets, researchers and practitioners are putting their best efforts in trying to raise awareness and train staff from the public and private institutions about the evolving nature of cyberspace threats. Several leading institutions from

© IFIP International Federation for Information Processing 2018
Published by Springer Nature Switzerland AG 2018. All Rights Reserved
L. Drevin and M. Theocharidou (Eds.): WISE 2018, IFIP AICT 531, pp. 40–54, 2018.
https://doi.org/10.1007/978-3-319-99734-6_4

academia and beyond have already paved the way for further research related to cyber security [2] (p. 21).

In line with recent developments, the Joint Task Force on Cybersecurity Education (JTF), created in September 2015, has developed a new curriculum volume, as part of its continuous efforts on the main purpose of developing comprehensive curriculum guidance in cyber security education [8]. The new curriculum volume introduces some new crosscutting concepts to deal with the evolving nature of cyberspace threats. These are:

- Adversarial thinking, as a process that considers the potential actions of the opposing force working against the desired result.
- Systems thinking, as a process that considers the interplay between social and technical constraints to enable assured operations.

The contribution of our work is directed towards the improvement of the adversarial and systems thinking ability in cyber security with focus on Master level students. This study was performed using an agent-based simulation tool, named CyberAIMs. The name is an acronym for Cyber Agents' Interactive Modeling and Simulation. It also shows that each actor in cyberspace follows certain procedures and strategies according to their own aims, as part of a higher entity or on individual basis. CyberAIMs was built using NetLogo[1], which is a programmable modeling environment for simulating natural and social phenomena. NetLogo is particularly well suited for modeling complex systems developing over time, with hundreds or thousands of agents, all operating independently.

We used this tool as the main component of a simulation-based experiment conducted with students of Information Security, in order to further address their adversarial and systems thinking abilities. The target group included 12 individuals in an elective Master course that were asked to answer two surveys, pre and post-experiment, as well as a scenario of a recent real-world case of a cyber attack during the experiment. Students were intended to use CyberAIMs in order to give correct answers to the questions from the scenario.

1.1 Learning Benefits

Pastor et al. [9] have done extensive research work on the available state-of-the art simulation tools that can be used on the purpose of teaching and training. They suggest that such simulation tools should be designed to have a extremely simple user-friendly interface and, at the same time, allow the user to obtain a deep understanding of the concepts.

Adversarial thinking has already been studied as an important skill for cyber security, Hamman et al. [7] propose that cyber security students should learn about basic game theory concepts in order to improve their strategic reasoning abilities. Similar to Schneider [12], our work aims to teach cyber security to students at university level.

---

[1] http://ccl.northwestern.edu/netlogo/.

Systems thinking has been associated to different areas of research since several decades now, and can also be relevant for information and cyber security. There are many examples where using simulations for teaching systems thinking, such as the work from Goodwin and Franklin [6], or the contribution from Anne Badoel and Haslett [3]. Their seminal work motivated our work further in this paper, while aiming to use simulation as part of the curriculum developed in the field of cyber security.

We aim to reflect the mechanisms behind the thinking processes above by using them within CyberAIMs, part of our recent research work done in the intersection between cyber security and related research fields.

1.2 Outline of the Paper

We have organized the paper contents as follows. Section 2 will provide information on the main research question and methodology used. Section 3 will provide more details on the design process of the tool used and its main features. The final sections will conclude this paper by providing main insights from the pilot study and relevant discussions to help the reader get familiar with the next objectives of this research process as a whole.

2   Research Methodology

2.1   Research Questions

The main aim of this paper is to produce a proof of concept artifact that is able to show how a simulation tool can affect thinking processes of a group of students in cyber security. With this artifact we hope to address the new directions suggested in developing curriculum for cyber security in education. We have devised the following research question in order to achieve the objectives mentioned above:

- Research Question (RQ): How can we improve adversarial and systems thinking ability on students in cyber security?

This research question helps us understand the approaches that might help improve the learning process of adversarial and/or systems thinking for training and teaching purposes, as mentioned above. We have proposed a simulation tool, inspired from the work of Pastor et al. [9], that may prove to be useful in such case. We justify the use of the simulation tool further in Sect. 4 by using the results from the pre-test/post-test study with the sample target. The process is explained in the next subsection below.

2.2   Research Methodology

Besides using a simulation tool as an intuitive way to improve learning outcomes of a cyber security course, we saw the need to validate potential outcomes by conducting surveys before and after the tool was used from the target sample.

The surveys included a set of similar questions and a set of different questions, according to the objectives of this study. Each student was asked to provide their ID as a means to uniquely identify them. The students were also asked if they wanted to receive via email a soft copy of their individual answers.

In the pre-simulation survey, there were three sections of open and closed questions, listed below:

- Learning from simulations
- About you
- Expectations from the model

In the first section, students were provided with two sets of statements and further asked to answer them using a 5-levelled Likert scale, with values ranging from strongly disagree to strongly agree. Table 1 gives details on all questions requiring Likert scale feedback from respondents.

Table 1. Pre-simulation survey questions using Likert scale

Section	Question	Statements/Options
Learning from simulations	I expect that the simulation will develop my	Problem solving skills; Planning skills; Understanding of cybercrime; Understanding of economics theories on cybercrime; Understanding of strategic mgmt. of info. security; Understanding of risk management; Understanding of real-world cyber scenarios; Understanding of systems thinking; Understanding of adversarial thinking
	Please rate your agreement with the following	The simulation will be challenging; I will enjoy learning with the simulation; Building on knowledge gained from previous courses; Building on knowledge gained from previous labs
About you	Please rate your agreement with the following	I have a background in programming; I have a background in economics/management; I have a background in human sciences/psychology; I have a background in military/warfare strategies
Expectations from the model	Please rate the level of relevance for each attribute on the attack success rate	Defense Resources; Defense Skills; Defense Motivation; Attack Resources; Attack Skills; Attack Motivation
	Please rate the level of relevance for each attribute on the defense success rate	Defense Resources; Defense Skills; Defense Motivation; Attack Resources; Attack Skills; Attack Motivation

The next section of this survey required feedback on the respondents current program of studies, home country, gender and age. It also included a question on the respondents' background using a Likert scale with same values as above.

The final section included two questions on the students' expectations related to the most relevant attributes. They had to provide answers using another 5-levelled Likert scale by rating all attributes given from highly irrelevant to highly relevant regarding their impact on each side's success rate, linked to the probability of the simulation ending in fewer steps than the maximum available ones. Students were further asked to rank top three attributes that they thought were most relevant. They had also the opportunity to submit optional comments on the rationale behind the answers provided in this section.

In order to simplify and improve the learning outcomes, we created a scenario related to a recent real-world case of a cyber attack, that could be easily mapped into CyberAIMs and further analyzed. The scenario was the main part of the lab conducted with the students, where they were asked to answer questions by putting into practice their knowledge on the tool and the logic behind the attributes involved. Questions included calculating the defense success rate and defining the most relevant attributes related to this rate. In the next section, we will provide more details about CyberAIMs.

The post-simulation survey included two sections of open and closed questions, similar to the first and last section of the pre-survey. The perspective changed from the expected to the real learning outcomes from using the tool. Here, in the final section, an additional question required respondents' feedback on the total time of engagement with the tool as well as a concluding optional comment on the whole experience related to the experiment.

3   CyberAIMs

CyberAIMs is an agent-based simulation tool designed in NetLogo, as shown in Fig. 1. It includes two sets of agents, namely defense and attack agents. We classified each of the groups in four distinct categories, hereinafter echelons.

Defense echelons are: *Ind* (individuals, ordinary people, related to a specific socio-cultural context), *SMB* (small and medium businesses, with relatively low yearly income), *Corp* (multinational corporations, biggest enterprises), *State* (state agents, part of high-level organizations and agencies).

Attack echelons are: *Kid* (the script kiddies, individual hackers, also part of a specific socio-cultural context), *Ideol* (ideological hackers, hack-tivists, acting on the basis on moral and ethical duty), *Contract* (the Contractors, organized cybercrime groups, providing illegitimate services in exchange for money or other incentives), *State* (state-sponsored attack agents, high-level organizations and agencies, heavily engaged in cyberwar events recently).

We defined further three attributes to explain the behaviour and performance of the agents within CyberAIMs. The attributes are *Resources*, the budget related to cyber activities; *Skills*, the level of training, literacy and awareness on cyber events; and *Motivation*, the level of self-motivation and incentives in a certain time.

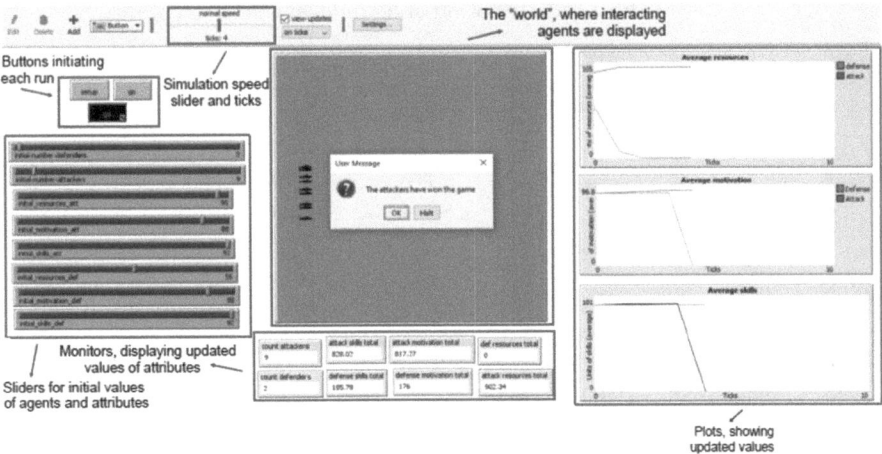

Fig. 1. Screenshot - CyberAIMs

We used various sources of data for *Resources* depending on the agents' side and echelons, including the Ponemon Report [10], and also the GCI Index [5] for the *Skills* units. As an example, an individual spending 1000 USD would have 25 units of *Resources*, while a state spending USD 1 billion would have 75 units. Meanwhile, agents from Singapore, the country with the highest GCI score, would have on average 92 units of *Skills*. Finally, we used a heuristic approach for *Motivation* in this version of CyberAIMs, which only included a four-levelled scale from Low to High. In the next versions of the tool, we intend to use various motivation theories, as explained in the last section.

The current version of CyberAIMs allows the user to define initial number of agents in each side of the battlefield and also the initial value for each of the attributes for all agents on each side. The user can choose values in a [1 100] range for the number of agents on each side, initial units of *Resources* and *Motivation*, and a [1, 93] range for the *Skills* units, as detailed in Table 2.

The tool performs each run in a period of max 120 ticks. Each tick represents a fixed period of time of three days, mapping the minimum time required for an attacker to perform a successful attack [10], thus making it able to predict the behavior of agents on both sides within a year. The current version allows a random attack agent on each tick to randomly target one or more defense agents, while attacking them depends on the combined attributes' values on each side.

If the attack is performed, the defense agent on target loses to the attacking agent a certain amount of *Resources*, related to the attack agent's relative power, defined by multiplying the latter attribute values and dividing them by the sum of attribute values' products from both agents. The *Skills* units are also updated by increasing values in both sides, with the defense agent having a larger increase in terms of learning experience. *Motivation* units are also updated on the attack agent's side, increasing them by the value of its relative power. If the attack is

Table 2. Distribution of attributes' values

Attribute	Side	Echelon/Level	Range of values
Resources	Defense	Ind	1–31
		SMB	1–40
		Corp	40–70
		State	60–100
	Attack	Kid	1–37
		Ideol	15–37
		Contract	35–67
		State	60–100
Skills	Attack/Defense	Low	1–30
		Medium	31–70
		High	71–93
Motivation	Attack/Defense	Low	1–25
		Moderate low	26–50
		Medium	51–75
		High	76–100

avoided, *Motivation* units are updated only on the defense side, by the value of the attack agent's relative power.

Continuous successful attacks can actually decrease defense agents' *Resources* units until losing them all. When this happens, the defense agent goes offline, meaning he does not interact anymore with the other agents. When all defense agents go offline, CyberAIMs stops running, displaying a message on the attack agents winning the game, as in Fig. 1 above.

By having initial values of attributes comparable between them along with successful attacks defined by the simple product of attributes values, CyberAIMs aims to analyze the impact of initially equal attributes in the final outcome after each run. Furthermore, changing *Skills* and *Motivation* values along with *Resources* values helps create a more holistic approach to the problem in question. This is how we aimed to reflect the systems thinking concept within the tool, while *Resources* are more relevant only when comparing outcomes between attack agents of different echelons, with values of *Skills* and *Motivation* kept constant.

In terms of adversarial thinking, CyberAIMs allows the attack agents to decide if they want to attack their target opponents based on their attribute values. Thus, attack agents have full information on their opponents before taking the next step and they are able to think like their potential targets.

4 Study Results

The target sample was composed from 12 students, attending the same course, while studying in several Masters' programs. Students had two hours of introduction to the tool developed, including the emerging concepts in cyber security curriculum related to systems and adversarial thinking. They were then asked to answer a pre-survey, followed by a scenario of a recent real-world case of a cyber attack during the experiment, and then the post-experiment survey.

4.1 Pre-simulation Survey

We received seven surveys completed out of 12 (58,3% response rate) that will be part of the analysis below. The gender composition was two female and five male respondents. The age range of the respondents included values from 23 to 54 years old and the respondents were part of four different Masters' programs. Three students were non native, one of them being an exchange student.

Five students had a programming background, while one of them had it combined with a background in management or economics and another one had also a background in psychology or human sciences. Only one respondent had a strong military background and that was combined with a strong background in management or economics as well.

Regarding questions from the first section, six students expected the tool could help them develop their understanding of adversarial thinking and four of them agreed on the statement about systems thinking. On the other hand, only one student expected the simulation would develop his understanding on risk management.

Six students thought that the simulation would be challenging, while five of them thought they would enjoy learning with the simulation. Five students expected the simulation would build on knowledge from previous courses, while only three of them expected it would build on previous labs they attended.

In the last section, respondents answered that the defense *Motivation* was the least relevant attribute for the attack success rate, while attack *Resources* was the least relevant attribute for the defense success rate. The results show that the most relevant attributes affecting the attack success rate were *Motivation* and *Skills* of attack side and then *Resources* for the defense side. On the other side, the most relevant attributes expected to affect defense success rate were defense *Resources*, *Skills* and then *Motivation*.

Results from the first and last section were compared with results coming from the scenarios and post-simulation survey where appropriate.

4.2 Scenario Results

The scenario was the main output of the lab conducted with the students, and we received answers from eight respondents out of 12 (66% response rate).

We prepared the scenario based on a real cyber case occurred recently, where an Iranian state-sponsored group was successful in targeting critical infrastructure entities in the US, Saudi Arabia and South Korea[2].

Thus, building on this real case, we asked the students to analyze these results using the simulation tool and values mapped from the actors participating there.

First, we instructed students on using the values shown in Table 3 to define initial units of *Resources* and *Skills* for each country or entity that was part of the scenario.

Table 3. Relevant values for the scenario

Entity/Country	Resources	Skills
US	98	91
Saudi Arabia	90	57
South Korea	88	78
Iran	84	49
Corporations	40–70	1–100

The values for the *Resources* are mostly related to the State agents' values for each country, considering the companies were part of the critical infrastructure. Table 3 also includes values related to agents representing multinational corporations, since they could reflect same behavior with the ones targeted in the real attack. We suggested the *Skills* values above in order to think how the tool could help analyze the event explained in the scenario by using respective values from the GCI index, but we instructed the students on the best approach being to use distributed values of *Skills* and *Motivation* on both sides, so as to reflect the random distribution of values among different agents.

In the first question, we asked the students about the success rate of the defense agents involved in this scenario, whether they represented US, Saudi, Korean or corporations entities. The answers are summarized in Fig. 2 the chart below.

The second question asked the respondents to submit initial attribute values on both sides for at least three cases when the attack agents succeeded in their attempts to win the battle, followed by at least three cases when the defense agents succeeded in their attempt to avoid being attacked. This question was considered relevant so as to make respondents think about potential patterns drawn from the values shown here and possible correlations between attributes and the final outcome in terms of each side's success as above. It was also useful in understanding how well the respondents followed the instructions given in the first question.

Following the same logic, the third question asked respondents to rank up to three of the six defined attributes (three on each side) as the most relevant ones

---

[2] https://thehackernews.com/2017/09/apt33-iranian-hackers.html.

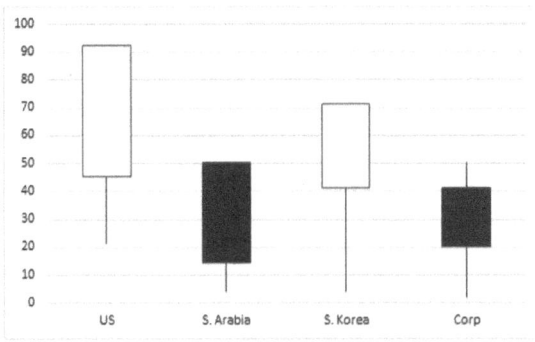

Fig. 2. Defense success rate (%) - responses

affecting the chances of a defense agent to survive the whole run of 120 ticks, thus his overall success rate. The results were quite different from the same question posed in the pre-simulation survey. They showed defense *Motivation* as the most relevant attribute, followed by defense *Skills* and then attack *Motivation*. Defense *Resources* was ranked fourth overall, thus a quite different outcome from the pre-survey, while a larger sample size would provide more meaningful results on this case.

4.3 Post-simulation Survey

We have received only four surveys completed out of 12 (33% response rate) for the post-simulation phase, while a more detailed analysis will be part of the future stages of our research.

In the first section, two respondents stated that CyberAIMs developed their understanding of economic theories in cybercrime, while the others agreed on the simulation developing their own understanding of cybercrime. Three respondents agreed on the simulation developing their understanding on strategic management of information security, and two of them stated that the simulation developed their risk management knowledge.

Three respondents agreed that the simulation developed their understanding of real world cyber scenarios. Regarding the main objective of this simulation-based experiment on learning outcomes, two out of four respondents agreed that the simulation did develop their understanding on systems thinking and, again, only two of them agreed on the statement about adversarial thinking.

All respondents thought that the simulation was challenging and that they enjoyed learning with it. Only one respondent agreed on the simulation building on knowledge from previous courses and another one agreed on the statement regarding previous labs, with the other respondents not agreeing or being neutral.

In the last section, when asked about the level of relevance of all attributes in the attack success rate, the respondents agreed that the most relevant one is attack *Motivation*. The other attributes in the top three were attack *Skills* and defense *Motivation*.

On the other hand, when asked about the most relevant attributes on the defense success rate, all respondents seemed to agree on the most relevant attribute being attack *Motivation*, followed by defense *Motivation* and then defense *Skills*.

The current results from this section, even in this preliminary stage, could define a change in perspective between the pre-study and the post-study, supported from the lab conducted using the tool.

Meanwhile, the results from the question on the respondents' engagement with the tool show that respondents spent a total time between four to five hours on learning CyberAIMs and creating useful outputs from it. Thus, somewhat between one and two regular lecture sessions were seemingly enough to change their perspective as related to systems and adversarial thinking, though a larger sample size is needed to produce statistically more significant results on this direction.

5   Discussion and Conclusions

Only three cases were valid for the whole process from the first to the second survey out of a total of 12 students in the course (25% rate). The answers on the most relevant attributes affecting defense success rate were the only connecting dots, while Table 4 shows the different responses before and after using CyberAIMs.

Table 4. Most relevant attributes on the defense success rate

Pre-survey responses	Post-survey responses
Defense *Resources*	Attack *Motivation*
Defense *Skills*	Defense *Motivation*
Defense *Motivation*	Defense *Skills*

Overall results reflect a better understanding of systems thinking, in terms of considering as most relevant attributes *Motivation* and *Skills* instead of *Resources* of each side, along with a better understanding of adversarial thinking, while thinking of attack attributes as equal or more relevant than defense ones on the defense side performance.

5.1   Additional Comments

The results above are prone to additional implications. Only four students were able to compute decreasing success rates of the defense side between the scenarios in the first question. According to their comments on the results, it seems that two of them were not able to follow our instructions on how to perform the analysis, while the two others could not apply them in the correct way.

The respondents further enforced these issues in their comments on the final survey, establishing a potential direction for further improvements in the whole process.

There were also useful comments received on the tool itself, including its design and the underlying features and values' distribution of the attributes, which is already incorporated in the forthcoming version of CyberAIMs, part of the future research.

5.2 Conclusions

This paper aims to contribute on recent research done in respect to the learning benefits of simulation tools in cyber security education. The main outcomes of our pilot study point to a shift of the respondents' perspective after using the tool, indicating that CyberAIMs can have an effect on the students' understanding of systems and adversarial thinking. The results are however preliminary, while this tool will be further improved and designed to be used for larger sample sizes of students in related programs of study and potential cyber competitions.

We are already designing another version of CyberAIMs, using another approach towards a more realistic picture of the current cyberspace, based on the work of Ablon et al. in [1]. Furthermore, we intend to look deeper into the *Motivation* attribute, through a more detailed literature review on the underlying theories, such as the MOMM's taxonomy [4] and the protection theory [11].

We intend to use the feedback received from the overall process in order to increase response rates and increase the usability and coverage levels of the forthcoming versions of CyberAIMs.

Appendix

A1. Pre-simulation Survey

Student ID number: _____
Note: this information will only be used to link your pre-simulation and post-simulation surveys and will not be retained for further analysis.

SECTION 1: LEARNING FROM SIMULATIONS
This section aims to get information on a 5-levelled Likert scale (strongly disagree - strongly agree) basis, according to your own perceptions and expectations. The Likert scale will be replaced by numbers, as follows:

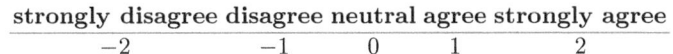

strongly disagree	disagree	neutral	agree	strongly agree
−2	−1	0	1	2

1. I expect that the simulation will develop my:

	−2	−1	0	1	2
problem solving skills					
planning skills					
understanding of cybercrime					
understanding of economics theories on cybercrime					
understanding of strategic mgmt. of info. security					
understanding of risk management					
understanding of real-world cyber scenarios					
understanding of systems thinking					
understanding of adversarial thinking					

2. Please rate your agreement with the following statements:

	−2	−1	0	1	2
The simulation will be challenging					
I will enjoy learning with the simulation					
It will build on knowledge gained from previous groups					
It will build on knowledge gained from previous labs					

SECTION 2: ABOUT YOU
This section will require some personal information from you

1. Please tell us your gender:
   - Female
   - Male
   - Prefer not to answer
2. In what year were you born? ____
3. If you are an international student, what is your home country? _____
4. What is the name of the degree you are completing? _____
5. Which of the following apply to you? (Select all that apply)

   - I am studying part-time
   - *I am studying externally (distance education)*
   - *English is not my first language*
   - *I am an International student*
   - *I am working casually / part-time while studying*
   - *I am working full-time while studying*
   - *I am an exchange student*

6. Please rate your agreement with the following statements:

	-2	-1	0	1	2
I have a background in programming					
I have a background in economics or management sciences					
I have a background in human sciences/psychology					
I have a background in military/warfare strategies and rules					

SECTION 3: EXPECTATIONS FROM THE MODEL
This section requires information on your perceptions and expectations on a 5-levelled Likert scale (highly irrelevant - highly relevant) basis, related to the model features explained before the lab. The Likert scale will be replaced by numbers, as follows:

highly irrelevant	**irrelevant**	**neutral**	**relevant**	**highly relevant**
0	1	2	3	4

1. Please rate the level of relevance for each attribute on the attack/defense success rate:

Attack	0	1	2	3	4	Defense	0	1	2	3	4
Defense Resources						*Defense Resources*					
Defense Skills						*Defense Skills*					
Defense Motivation						*Defense Motivation*					
Attack Resources						*Attack Resources*					
Attack Skills						*Attack Skills*					
Attack Motivation						*Attack Motivation*					

2. What do you expect to be the top 3 attributes for the attack agents' success rate?

Example: a. attack resources; b. defense skills; c. defense resources;

a. _____
b. _____
c. _____

3. What is the rationale behind your selection above?
_____
_____
_____

4. What do you expect to be the top 3 attributes for the defense agents' success rate?

Example: a. attack resources; b. defense skills; c. defense resources;

a. _____
b. _____
c. _____

5. What is the rationale behind your selection above?

Thank you for your participation!

References

1. Ablon, L., Libicki, M.C., Golay, A.A.: Markets for cybercrime tools and stolen data: hackers' bazaar. Rand Corporation (2014)
2. ACM: Computer Science Curricula 2013 Curriculum Guidelines for Undergraduate Degree Programs in Computer Science. New York, NY, USA (2013)
3. Anne Bardoel, E., Haslett, T.: Success to the successful: the use of systems thinking tools in teaching OB. Organ. Manag. J. **1**(2), 112–124 (2004)
4. Bologna, J.: Momm's (motivations, opportunities, methods, means)-a taxonomy for computer related employee theft. Assets Prot. **6**(3), 33–36 (1981)
5. Brahima, S.: Global cybersecurity index 2017. International Telecommunication Union (ITU), pp. 1–77 (2017)
6. Goodwin, J.S., Franklin, S.G.: The beer distribution game: using simulation to teach systems thinking. J. Manag. Dev. **13**(8), 7–15 (1994)
7. Hamman, S.T., Hopkinson, K.M., Markham, R.L., Chaplik, A.M., Metzler, G.E.: Teaching game theory to improve adversarial thinking in cybersecurity students. IEEE Trans. Educ. **60**(3), 205–211 (2017)
8. Joint Task Force on Cybersecurity Education: Cybersecurity curricula 2017 - curriculum guidelines for post-secondary degree programs in cybersecurity - csec2017 v. 0.95 draft. Technical report, November 2017
9. Pastor, V., Díaz, G., Castro, M.: State-of-the-art simulation systems for information security education, training and awareness. In: 2010 IEEE Education Engineering (EDUCON), pp. 1907–1916. IEEE (2010)
10. Ponemon Institute: Flipping the economics of attacks. Technical report, January 2016
11. Rogers, R.W.: A protection motivation theory of fear appeals and attitude change1. J. Psychol. **91**(1), 93–114 (1975)
12. Schneider, F.B.: Cybersecurity education in universities. IEEE Secur. Priv. **11**(4), 3–4 (2013)

Information Security Training and Awareness

Towards Educational Guidelines
for the Security Systems Engineer

Suné von Solms[1][(✉)] ⓘ and Annlizé Marnewick[2]

[1] Department of Electrical Engineering Science,
University of Johannesburg, Johannesburg, South Africa
svonsolms@uj.ac.za
[2] Postgraduate School of Engineering Management,
University of Johannesburg, Johannesburg, South Africa

Abstract. Industry 4.0 will impact the systems engineering landscape and cybersecurity in the future. The education needs of system engineers working in these environments will change as the system landscape adapt to the Industry 4.0 changes. This research aims to explore the impact of Industry 4.0 on systems engineering and security requirements which must be catered for in future in this changing Industry 4.0 landscape. Although it is not certain yet how the landscape will change, this research starts to explore what the potential education needs could be for system engineers to understand all future cybersecurity requirements. The results of this research indicate that security requirements engineering will be needed in the first requirements stage of the systems development life cycle. Secondly, a new set of expert engineering skills will be required to identify future threats and vulnerabilities which could impact the system landscape. These results can be used as a guideline to start thinking how system engineers should be educated for the future.

Keywords: Engineering education · Security
Security requirements engineering · Industry 4.0 · Systems engineering

1 Introduction

The rise of Industry 4.0, also referred to as the Industrial Internet of Things (IIoT) or the fourth industrial revolution, defines the use of new digitized and connected industrial systems, assumed to yield extensive industry-spanning opportunities [1]. These new systems are expected to be smart cyber-physical systems which communicate and work with other systems and humans in real time [2]. The interconnected nature of Industry 4.0–driven operations and systems means that the impact and effects of cyberattacks on these systems will be more extensive on the engineering systems than before [3].

The fear of industry and academia is that the designers, manufacturers and their supply networks may not be prepared for the risks that these Industry 4.0–driven systems presents. This posts one of the biggest challenges for engineering design and also for engineering education [3, 4]. To address these uncertainties, the engineering space has recently seen a large drive to include extensive cybersecurity processes into

L. Drevin and M. Theocharidou (Eds.): WISE 2018, IFIP AICT 531, pp. 57–68, 2018.
https://doi.org/10.1007/978-3-319-99734-6_5

systems engineering process requirements engineering. This is due to the traditional systems engineering processes being inadequate for the development of secure systems, as cybersecurity had less impact on business operations as the environment were isolated versus the new connected environment [5, 6]. In the past, security integration in engineering systems was limited to the IT industry, where security were added after the completed system was developed. However, with the new drive for integration, security must be included in software development, risk management, human factors and all other areas within an organization [7, 8]. The International Council of Systems Engineering (INCOSE) has chartered a working group in 2016 to start the processes required for fostering security within systems engineering, where system security is "accepted and practiced as a fundamental part of system engineering" [5] and where security is incorporated across the entire systems development lifecycle [9, 10].

There exist limited studies in the field of systems engineering that aim to investigate how the cybersecurity knowledge and skills of the systems engineer in the industrial workforce are changing. This research aims to investigate the additional cybersecurity-related activities the systems engineer will be responsible for in order to design Industry 4.0-ready systems. As the range of cybersecurity activities are so wide-ranging throughout the design of engineering systems, this paper will only consider the activities in the Requirements and Conceptualization phase of an engineering project.

2 Overview of the Current Systems Engineering Landscape

The increased connectivity of smart systems essential for Industry 4.0 requires the design of smart, autonomous technologies. These connected, smart systems, aiming to fully integrate the digital and physical world, introduce a new set of cyber risks. The interconnected nature of these systems requires organizations to employ professionals with the skills and competencies to design Industry 4.0–ready systems. For cyber risks to be adequately addressed, cybersecurity strategies should be fully integrated into organizational and design strategies from the start [3].

When designing traditional systems, the systems engineer would typically leave the cybersecurity aspects of a system to the security professionals [5]. In many cases the security features of a system were treated as of secondary importance. One of the main work roles of the systems engineer is to derive a complete set of functional requirements (criteria defining specific behavior and functions) and non-functional requirements (criteria indicating the operation and constraints) of the system. Security is generally considered a non-functional requirement and are typically considered less important than functional requirements [5, 6]. It is stated by Dove et al. [5] that "as long as systems engineers do not consider security a functional requirement, it will not be likely to rise to the top of the implementation checklist". To address this issue, INCOSE admits that new approaches to systems engineering will need to be implemented in order to meet the need for secure systems in the era of Industry 4.0 [5].

The National Institute of Standards and Technology (NIST) produced the National Initiative for Cybersecurity Education (NICE) Cybersecurity Workforce Framework in August 2017 which highlights the need for interdisciplinary nature of cybersecurity work and provides guidance on workforce development, training and education of cybersecurity professionals [11]. This includes information regarding cybersecurity-related activities and tasks of an organization and the relevant work role responsible for each activity or task. It also details the knowledge, abilities and skills required by a professional in order to successfully execute the applicable tasks and activities [6, 11–15]. As the updating of the systems engineering framework by INCOSE to include cybersecurity is still a work in progress, the NICE Cybersecurity Workforce Framework publication is currently used to evaluate the inclusion of cybersecurity considerations in the system development life cycle (SDLC) of systems engineering.

Due to the limited exposure of systems engineers to cybersecurity, many systems engineers lack the knowledge, abilities and skills required to address potential Industry 4.0-related security issues. This lack in cybersecurity knowledge regarding security risk analysis, as well as the lack in vision to consider systems and their threats/risks in their entirety leads to gaps in the security architecture of systems [6, 16].

3 Methodology

This work analyses the activities in the traditional systems development life cycle (SDLC) as well as the updated secure systems development life cycle (S-SDLC) to determine the additional cybersecurity activities required by the process and where the responsibilities lie. As the range of cybersecurity activities are so wide-ranging, this paper will only consider the activities in the Requirements and Conceptualization phase of an engineering project. The research presented in this paper aims to determine the new activities that a systems engineer will be exposed to when developing systems for the Industry 4.0 environment. This work comments on the potential activities and responsibilities shortfall amongst traditional systems engineers in the era of Industry 4.0. The methodology followed consists of the following steps:

1. To conduct a content analysis on the traditional SDLC processes captured by the ISO/ICE/IEEE 15288:2015 [17] standard to identify the range of security activities included in the SDLC and where the responsibility lies.
2. To conduct a content analysis on the NIST NICE Cybersecurity Workforce Framework [11] to determine the proposed cybersecurity related activities required in the S-SDLC and where the responsibility lies.
3. Comment on the activities, knowledge, abilities and skills differences between the two processes and determine the how the role of the systems engineer in the industrial workforce might change.

The results of the various steps are discussed in the subsequent sections.

4 Analysis of Security Activities in the SDLC

4.1 Responsibilities of the Systems Engineer in the SDLC

When a new system is developed, a coordination of numerous activities and processes from a collection of professionals are required. The systems engineer's responsibility starts with the need of a new system or problem that must be solved, and ends when the system is operational and used by end-users or customers. The responsibility of the systems engineer would be based on individual experience, systems engineering knowledge and current system complexity. One of the main work roles of the systems engineer is to derive a complete set of functional and non-functional requirements of the system. This requirements engineering process uses the results of risk analysis and threat assessments as goals that must be met by the system to initialize the elicitation activity [15]. This risk analysis and threat assessment is traditionally the responsibility of a systems engineer. In the traditional SDLC, the goal of the risk management processes, according to Parnell et al. [18], is to identify, assess and take action to reduce risks of system technical performance, cost and schedule estimates. However, the analysis and assessment of extreme risks, including cybersecurity, is not traditionally seen as the systems engineer's responsibility but rather an expert risk analyst [19].

Sage and Rouse [19] states the following responsibilities of a systems engineer relating to requirements engineering:

1. Need identification and customer linkage: the need is identified through the matching of the need with the technical feasibility and provide the linkage between the customer's needs and the design of the system.
2. Requirements management: the customer needs is developed as in input to determine the systems and functional requirements.
3. Architecture and systems design: design the system's concept and link the requirements with the configuration.
4. Technical risk and management: perform a technical risk assessment and manage these risks during trade-off analysis.

It can be seen that no direct mention is made of any security related responsibilities. Traditionally, when designing systems, the systems engineer would leave the cybersecurity aspects of a system to the security professionals [5].

4.2   Overview of the SDLC

In industry, systems engineers utilize best practice systems engineering processes and methods to execute the activities during system development. System development progresses through the life cycle stages, and make use of decision gates to determine the way forward [20]. This discovery process is generally structured into stages throughout the system life cycle where it is conceptualize, developed, produced, utilized, supported and retired [18]. Figure 1 illustrates a generic systems engineering life cycle as described by ISO/IEC/IEEE 15288:2015.

| System concept development stage | Design and development stage | Production stage | Development stage | Retirement stage |
| | | | System operations | |

Fig. 1. Generic Systems engineering generic life cycle [16, 18]

The process model followed by a systems team depends on prior experience of the resources and standard approaches used by the organization or problem type to be solved, therefore there does not exist one SDLC for all engineering systems [19]. Comparisons of the available life cycle models used by various organizations or disciplines are available in literature [18, 20]. A typical SDLC used in a commercial systems integrator environment is illustrated in Fig. 2.

System concept development stage			Design and development stage				Production stage	Development stage	Retirement stage
								System operations	
Requirements and conceptualization phase			Implementation period					Operations period	
User requirement phase	Concept definition	System specification	Acquisition preparation phase	Selection phase	Development phase	Verification phase	Deployment phase	Operations & maintenance	Deactivation phase

Fig. 2. Typical SDLC for commercial systems integrator environments

During the SDLC stages shown in Fig. 2, the processes prescribed by standards and systems engineering communities are invoked [20]. The processes currently included in the body of knowledge do not directly include a process relating to security. In order to determine where the security-related activities are included in the systems engineering process, a content analysis is performed on the ISO/ICE/IEEE 15288:2015 framework, described in the subsequent section.

4.3   Content Analysis of Security in Systems Engineering Processes

A content analysis was performed on the ISO/IEC/IEEE 15288 2015 - Systems and software engineering - Systems life cycle processes document. The search term "security" was used in order to determine where security-related actions are included in the SDLC and who the responsible professionals are. Security activities show to impact three processes shown in Table 1.

Table 1. Results of content analysis of ISO/IEC/IEEE 15288 2015.

Search phrase	Results	Process	Comment on content
Security	3	Agreement process	Security is noted as an increasing concern. ISO/IEC 27036 is referred to for guidance how to secure information in supplier relationships
		Infrastructure management process	ISO/IEC 27036 is referred to for guidance how to secure outsourced infrastructure
		Project planning process	ISO/ICE 15026 and ISO/IEC 27036 is referred to for guidance related to ISO/IEC 27036 objectives and constraints related to assurance and security

It can be seen from the table that all the references to security in the document are references to other standards documents. It is noted in the ISO/ICE/IEE 15288 standard that "information security for supplier relationships" must be carefully considered [17]. It can be deduced from this analysis that the traditional SDLC does not include dedicated security activities. The systems engineering community acknowledged this lack and has responded with integration of security engineering into the systems engineering processes [14, 21, 22].

5   Analysis of Security Activities in the S-SDLC

5.1   Overview of the S-SDLC

The systems engineering community is in the process to identify security roles and responsibilities applicable to the entire systems development life cycle for future connected environments [21]. Various researchers have developed S-SDLC suggestions to show how and where security can be included in the S-SDLC. In these suggestions, security is included throughout the systems development life cycle stages. The first step in the proposed S-SDLC is the introduction of a new security requirements engineering process which is a sub process of the traditional requirements engineering activity [15]. The S-SDLC, illustrated in Fig. 3, indicates the updated Requirements and Conceptualization phase to illustrate the addition of the security requirements engineering process.

Requirements and conceptualization phase				Implementation period			Operations period		
User requirement phase	Concept definition	System specification	Acquisition preparation phase	Selection phase	Development phase	Verification phase	Deployment phase	Operations & maintenance	Deactivation phase
Risk Analysis	Risk assessment								
Security requirements engineering									

Fig. 3. S-SDLC indicating the addition of risk analysis and assessment relating to security requirements engineering

This security requirements engineering process's purpose is to elicit the security requirements the system should cater for in order to reduce risk [23]. The new security requirements engineering process is depended on a security risk analysis and assessment activity to derive a complete set of requirements [6, 15].

The goal of the security risk analysis is to identify potential sources of threats or vulnerabilities the new system could have. The risks identified must then be assessed to determine the potential impact on the organizations operations, assets, individuals and other implications [24]. The result of the risk assessment is then used as an input to the security requirements engineering process. The results are analyzed to identify suitable security requirements that can mitigate the potential threats and vulnerabilities within the organization's risk management strategy [15].

5.2   Responsibilities of the Systems Engineer

The literature states that the security requirements engineering process will in future potentially be integrated with the requirements activity as the systems engineer is generally the person with the holistic view of the system. This will require the systems engineer to develop the knowledge, competencies and skills in order to do complete security requirements.

The risk assessment and threat analysis activities, required as an input to the new security requirements engineering process, are additional activities not previously included within the system engineering responsibility. Traditionally, the risk analysis performed by the systems engineer did not include activities relating to security and only considered technical risk assessment, as discussed in Sect. 4.1. For the system engineer to perform the new security risk analysis and threat assessment, he/she will require new knowledge, competencies and skills.

If the systems engineer is not the professional who will take responsibility for these tasks, these tasks must become the responsibility of another cybersecurity professional. In order to determine the responsible professional(s) for these security-related activities, a content analysis was performed on the NIST NICE Cybersecurity Workforce Framework [10], described in the subsequent section.

5.3   Content Analysis of Security in S-SDLC

The NIST NICE Cybersecurity Workforce Framework describes an organization's cybersecurity needs by defining *Specialty Areas*, *Work Roles* and *Tasks*. Each specialty area represents an area of concentrated work, where each work role indicates the responsible person, and each task an activity. A range of steps were followed to determine who would be the professionals responsible for security-related risk assessment and requirement tasks according to the NIST NICE Cybersecurity Workforce Framework.

Step One. Who is responsible for the security requirements engineering tasks of the NIST cybersecurity framework? A content analysis was done of the phrase "security requirements" within the NICE Framework. The results relating to work roles are shown in Table 2 below.

Table 2. Results of content analysis on "security requirements" in NICE Cybersecurity Workforce Framework.

Search phrase	# results	Work role	Work role description
Security requirements	1	Security architect	Protects the organization's mission and that the business processes are adequately addressed in all aspects of enterprise architecture

Only one work role included the phrase "security requirements". Per definition, the Security Architect is not a work role which is included in the SDLC requirements and conceptualization phase. As a specific work role is not allocated for security requirements relating to the systems engineering and the SDLC, a second content analysis was done of the phrase "functional requirements" within the NICE Framework. The results are shown in Table 3 below.

Table 3. Results of content analysis on "functional requirements" in NICE Cybersecurity Workforce Framework.

Search phrase	# results	Work role	Work Role Description
Functional requirements	1	Systems requirements planner	Consults with customers to evaluate functional requirements and translate functional requirements into technical solutions

The framework only has one work role, namely Systems Requirements Planner, allocated to the tasks relating to functional requirements. As security requirements not listed as a separate function for the Systems Requirements Planner, it can be assumed that security requirements engineering activity remains the responsibility of the Systems Requirements Planner, which per definition relates to the systems engineer. Input to guide the security requirements engineering activity is the risk identification and assessment of all potential threats and vulnerabilities.

Step Two. Who is responsible for the risk analysis and threat assessment tasks of the NIST cybersecurity framework?

Content analysis was performed to identify who is responsible for risk analysis and threat assessment of the NIST cybersecurity framework. A search was done on the phrases "risk assessment", "assessment", "threat" and "vulnerabilities" within the NICE Framework. The results relating to work roles in the SDLC are shown in Table 4 below. From this result of this analysis, it can be seen that the work roles assigned for risk assessment includes the Security Control Assessor and Vulnerability Assessment Analyst. The Research and Development Specialist and the Exploitation Analyst are assigned to assess threats.

These roles are not roles traditionally defined in systems engineering processes, which would indicate that these are new roles required for the Industry 4.0 environment. Therefore, the S-SDLC will require a new type of engineer functioning as a Vulnerability Assessment Analyst and Exploitation Analyst who must perform the risk assessments and threat analysis activities. In the current environment a systems engineer developing the solution will not be able to take on these activities in addition to his/her existing work.

Table 4. Results of content analysis on "risk assessment", "assessment", "threat" and "vulnerabilities" in NICE Cybersecurity Workforce Framework.

Search phrase	Results	Work role	Work role description
Risk assessment	0	–	–
Assessment	2	Risk management - security control assessor	Conducts independent comprehensive assessments of the management, operational, and technical security controls and control enhancements employed within or inherited by an information technology (IT) system to determine the overall effectiveness of the controls
		Vulnerability assessment and management - vulnerability assessment analyst	Performs assessments of systems and networks within the network environment or enclave and identifies where those systems/networks deviate from acceptable configurations, enclave policy, or local policy. Measures effectiveness of defense-in-depth architecture against known vulnerabilities
Threat or vulnerabilities	3	Vulnerability assessment analyst	Duplication – see above
		Technology R&D (TRD) - research and development specialist	Conducts software and systems engineering and software systems research to develop new capabilities, ensuring cybersecurity is fully integrated. Conducts comprehensive technology research to evaluate potential vulnerabilities in cyberspace systems
		Exploitation analyst	Analyzes collected information to identify vulnerabilities and potential for exploitation

6   Discussion and Recommendations

System engineers cater for both physical and information security as part of the design [17], with the principle that the design of the system must prevent intentional introduction of faults with consequences of various impacts [25]. From this it is acknowledged that security is traditionally only considered and designed for the environment the system will operate in. As future environments will be much more connected, it has been highlighted that cybersecurity should be considered during the entire systems development lifecycle and not just bottom up during design and validation [26]. The analysis performed in Sect. 4 shows that there exist a clear need for the inclusion of cybersecurity-related activities in the SDLC. Cybersecurity skills related to security risk analysis, threat assessment and security requirements engineering, must be included in the systems engineering process.

Form the analysis done in Sect. 5, it can be seen that the cybersecurity-related activities added to the S-SLDC does not clearly indicate who the responsible person will be in a systems engineering context. It can then be argued that the additional cybersecurity-related activities may befall the systems engineer by default if no cybersecurity specialist is assigned to the process. The security risk analysis requires a holistic technical view, but also needs security risk scenario analysis and threat analysis skills, which most systems engineers do not currently possess.

The results of this study can pose the case for a new type of engineer to become an expert in the function of security risk analysis and threat assessment. The reason for this is that an engineer typically has a sound systems thinking ability to understand the holistic environment in order to identify all influences on the environment. An engineer capable of sound systems thinking skills as well as cybersecurity-related knowledge, skills and competencies relating to cybersecurity would form an important part of a systems engineering process in the future of Industry 4.0-ready systems. The requirement for this new type of systems engineer calls for the development of engineering education to include cybersecurity-related knowledge, skills and competencies into systems engineering curricula. Systems engineers need to be educated in the fields of security risk analysis and threat assessment, as well as security requirements engineering.

Currently, there only exist a hand full of known postgraduate cybersecurity engineering degrees worldwide, with even less of these focusing on cybersecurity within systems engineering. Two known Master's degrees include the Master of Science in Systems Engineering at Johns Hopkins Whiting School of Engineering [27] and the MS in Systems Engineering with Certificate in Cybersecurity University of Maryland, Baltimore County [28]. Currently no known postgraduate cybersecurity engineering degrees are offered by South African institutions [29]. The inclusion of cybersecurity in dedicated systems engineering modules and courses are even scarcer, leading to the existence of a mismatch between cybersecurity education in systems engineering and cybersecurity requirements from industry. Therefore, inclusion of cybersecurity in currently systems engineering courses or the creation of a cybersecurity systems engineering degree or postgraduate module is recommended.

7 Conclusion

This paper argues that in the light of Industry 4.0, there exist a need for the creation of systems with a greater level of connectivity, where cyberattacks on these systems may be more extensive than before [3]. It is therefore required by designers, manufacturers and supply networks to be prepared for the risks that these new Industry 4.0–driven systems presents.

This paper shows through content analyses that the current systems engineering processes do not consider all security activities needed in the light of the fourth industrial revolution. This paper also shows that when considering the new cybersecurity activities proposed to be included in the Requirements and Conceptualization phase of an engineering project, new cybersecurity-related knowledge and skills will be required. It is argued that these activities will require the addition of a systems engineer who possesses the knowledge, skills and competencies related to security risk analysis and threat assessment. As these knowledge and skills are not currently taught to systems engineers, it is argued that there exist a need in engineering education for the creation of such course or modules.

Future research would include an investigation on the identified cybersecurity-related activities and determine the relevant knowledge areas, abilities and skills required to successfully implement these activities. Future work must also consider other phases in the SDLC and determine the cybersecurity-related activities and where the responsibility lies. This work serves as a driver towards the creation of cybersecurity-related content into engineering education.

References

1. Kiel, A.: What do we know about "Industry 4.0" so far? In: Proceedings of the International Association for Management of Technology (IAMOT 2017) (2017)
2. Hermann, M., Pentek, T., Otto, B.: Design principles for Industrie 4.0 scenarios. In: 49th Hawaii International Conference on System Sciences (HICSS), pp. 3928–3937 (2016)
3. Waslo, R., Lewis, T., Hajj, R., Carton, R.: Industry 4.0 and cybersecurity: managing risk in an age of connected production. Deloitte University Press (2017). https://www2.deloitte.com/insights/us/en/focus/industry-4-0/cybersecurity-managing-risk-in-age-of-connected-production.html. Accessed 18 Apr 2018
4. Motyl, B., Baronio, G., Uberti, S., Speranza, D., Filippi, S.: How will change the future engineers' skills in the Industry 4.0 framework? A questionnaire survey. Procedia Manuf. **11**, 1501–1509 (2017)
5. Dove, R., Bayuk, J., Wilson, B., Kepchar, K.: INCOSE System Security Engineering Working Group Charter (2016). https://www.incose.org/docs/default-source/wgcharters/systems-security-engineering.pdf?sfvrsn=cc0eb2c6_8. Accessed 21 Apr 2018
6. Kim, Y.: Activities of security engineering in system development life cycle: security engineer's view. Presented at the 14th International Conference on Applications of Computer Engineering (ACE 2015), Seoul, South Korea, 5–7 September 2015
7. Shreyas, D.: Software Engineering for Security: Towards Architecting Secure Software (2001). http://citeseerx.ist.psu.edu/viewdoc/download?doi=10.1.1.3.4064&rep=rep1&type=pdf. Accessed 05 May 2018
8. Haridas, N.: Software Engineering – Security as a Process in the SDLC. SANS Institute InfoSec Reading Room (2007)
9. Morgan, S.: IBM's CEO on Hackers: Cyber Crime is the Greatest Threat to Every Company in the World (2015). https://www.forbes.com/sites/stevemorgan/2015/11/24/ibms-ceo-on-hackers-cyber-crime-is-the-greatest-threat-to-every-company-in-the-world/#1baf053373f0. Accessed 21 May 2018

10. Tamura, E.: Hewlett Packard Enterprise Leads Transformation of Cyber Defense with "Build it In" and "Stop it Now" (2016). http://www8.hp.com/us/en/hp-news/press-release.html?id=2184147#.WtlU5S6uyUl. Accessed 21 May 2018

11. Newhouse, W., Keith, S., Scribner, B., Witte, G.: National Initiative for Cybersecurity Education (NICE) cybersecurity workforce framework. In: Special Publication 800-181, NIST 2017 (2017)

12. Kissel, R.L., Stine, K.M., Scholl, M.A., Rossman, H., Fahlsing, J., Gulick, J.: Security considerations in the system development life cycle. In: NIST Special Publication 800-64, NIST 2018 (2018)

13. Dawson, M., Burrell, D., Rahim, E., Brewster, S.: Integrating software assurance into the Software Development Life Cycle (SDLC). J. Inf. Syst. Technol. Plan. 3(6), 49–53 (2010)

14. Mailloux, L.O., Garrison, C., Dove, R., Biondo, R.C.: Guidance for working group maintenance of the Systems Engineering Body of Knowledge (SEBoK) with systems security engineering example. In: INCOSE International Symposium, vol. 25, no. 1, pp. 1004–1019 (2015)

15. Salini, P., Kanmani, S.: Survey and analysis on security requirements engineering. Comput. Electr. Eng. **38**(6), 1785–1797 (2012)

16. Evans, S., Heinbuch, D., Kyle, E., Piorkowski, J., Wallner, J.: Risk-based systems security engineering: stopping attacks with intention. IEEE Secur. Priv. **2**(6), 59–62 (2004)

17. ISO, ISO/IEC/IEEE International Standard - Systems and software engineering – System life cycle processes. ISO/IEC/IEEE 15288 First edition 2015–05–15, pp. 1–118 (2015)

18. Parnell, G.S., Driscoll, P.J., Henderson, D.: Decision Making in Systems Engineering and Management. Systems Engineering and Management, p. 497. Wiley, Hoboken (2011)

19. Sage, A.P., Rouse, W.: Handbook of Systems Engineering and Management. Wiley Series in Systems Engineering and Management. Wiley, Chicester (2009)

20. Walden, D.D., Roedler, G.J., Forsberg, K.J., Hamelin, R.D., Shortell, T.M.: INCOSE Systems Engineering Handbook: A Guide for System Life Cycle Processes and Activities. Wiley, Hoboken (2015)

21. Nejib, P., Beyer, D., Yakabovicz, E.: Systems security engineering: what every system engineer needs to know. In: INCOSE International Symposium, vol. 27, no. 1, pp. 434–445 (2017)

22. Zemrowski, K.M.: NIST bases flagship security engineering publication on ISO/IEC/IEEE 15288:2015. Computer **49**(12), 86–88 (2016)

23. Türpe, S.: The trouble with security requirements. In: IEEE 25th International Requirements Engineering Conference (RE 2017), pp. 122–133 (2017)

24. National Institute of Standards and Technology (NIST), Guide for Conducting Risk Assessments, NIST 800-30 (2012)

25. Blanchard, B.S., Blyler, J.E.: System Engineering Management. Wiley, Hoboken (2016)

26. Bayuk, J.L., Horowitz, B.M.: An architectural systems engineering methodology for addressing cyber security. Syst. Eng. **14**(3), 294–304 (2011)

27. Johns Hopkins Whiting School of Engineering, Systems Engineering. https://ep.jhu.edu/programs-and-courses/programs/systems-engineering. Accessed 26 July 2018

28. University of Maryland, Baltimore County, Systems Engineering. http://se.umbc.edu/mssecyber.php. Accessed 26 July 2018

29. von Solms, S., Futcher, L.: Towards the design of a cybersecurity module for postgraduate engineering studies. In: Eleventh International Symposium on Human Aspects of Information Security and Assurance (HAISA 2017), Adelaide, Australia (2017)

The Feasibility of Raising Information Security Awareness in an Academic Environment Using SNA

Rudi Serfontein(iD), Lynette Drevin$^{(\boxtimes)}$(iD), and Hennie Kruger(iD)

North-West University, Potchefstroom, South Africa
{rudi.serfontein,lynette.drevin,
hennie.kruger}@nwu.ac.za

Abstract. The human aspect is one of the key success factors in information security (InfoSec). Its impact on InfoSec is so significant that multiple studies have shown that a balanced approach combining technology and security awareness is needed in order to maintain the integrity of an organisation's security. At present, one of the methods most often used to address InfoSec awareness is to develop security awareness programmes that can be used to educate its users within an organisation. This method has several drawbacks; however, as such programmes might not be comprehensive enough, or quick enough to address newer threats. It can furthermore lead to the users developing InfoSec fatigue, which renders most attempts at improving security awareness pointless. These problems are compounded by non-traditional organisational structures, such as those found in educational institutions, where both students and staff should be made aware of information security risks on a regular basis. In order to address the potential information security awareness problem at educational institutions, this paper investigates the feasibility of using Social Network Analysis (SNA) to improve existing security awareness programmes. Following a brief introduction to SNA, two illustrative examples are offered to show that SNA presents a viable option to improve programmes for raising information security awareness in an academic environment, by allowing for the effective selection of ideal target locations.

Keywords: Social network analysis · Security awareness · Security fatigue

1 Introduction

In the field of information security, one of the primary success factors is the human aspect [1]. Past research has shown that a balanced approach in which both techno-logical and social aspects are addressed is crucial to maintaining information security [2–4]. Despite repeated campaigns to educate users regarding information security, however, a significant number of users still engage in risky online behaviour [5] and are still considered the weakest link in information security [6]. Among the many places that can be negatively impacted by a lack of information security awareness, few are as vulnerable as universities. This stems from the fact that university networks need to be accessible to a wide variety of people, such as students, faculty members,

L. Drevin and M. Theocharidou (Eds.): WISE 2018, IFIP AICT 531, pp. 69–80, 2018.
https://doi.org/10.1007/978-3-319-99734-6_6

administrative staff, and visitors [4]. With the massive number and types of people that need to be able to access a university network, it is only reasonable to assume that a significant number of users will act in a way that compromises both the security of the university and their own personal security. One of the best known traditional methods of addressing this risk and educating users is security awareness programmes [7–9]. There are, however, a number of significant drawbacks to these awareness programmes, e.g. the awareness programmes might not be comprehensive enough [10], they might not address new threats quickly enough when the risks change continuously [11], and the programmes rely upon the users to consciously decide to comply with information security principles [12]. A significant amount of research is focused on attempting to address these shortcomings [13]. Another factor that may impact negatively on security awareness training is security fatigue. Security fatigue is a specific form of mental fatigue, which is a well-known phenomenon in psychology that describes the feeling a person has during or after prolonged periods of cognitive activity [14, 15]. Security fatigue is experienced by users when they are bombarded with information security knowledge to such a degree that they become overburdened with the information and may choose to abandon all conscious efforts to adhere to the security principles as explained during the course of the awareness programmes [16].

Given the importance of the human aspect in information security and the potential problems with broad security awareness programmes, an adaptive approach is proposed. In this paper, the feasibility of using Social Network Analysis (SNA) as a technique to positively influence information security awareness programmes, specifically those that are targeted at an academic environment, will be discussed. SNA is a method used to graphically represent a social organisation, such as a community or business, in such a way that the social interactions can be studied quantitatively [17]. The technique is suitable for use in environments where certain risks, including those risks associated with information security, are present, and has been used in the past to, among others:

- Identify core members and organisations within terrorist groups [18]; and
- Identify hierarchies in criminal Dark Web forums [19].

In addition to the studies mentioned above, SNA has also been used to enhance the information security of an organisation. The work done by Dang-Pham, Pittayachawan and Bruno [20] is of particular interest to this study as it serves to demonstrate the validity of the method discussed here. In the study done by Dang-Pham, Pittayachawan and Bruno, SNA was used to identify individuals who would be able to serve as information security champions. These individuals were then trained in information security so that their influence would help to shape the workplace culture with regards to information security. Because of the importance of this method, it will be referred to as the DPA-method (Dang-Pham Awareness) in the remainder of the paper. SNA has also been used in different studies to identify individuals who pose an organisational risk. By calculating the relative SNA metrics for the various nodes, individuals who may pose a risk due to their position in the network can be identified [21, 22].

The purpose of this paper is to address the information security awareness short-comings that may exist in university classes and faculties by employing an SNA approach. As the method can be applied to target important individuals and locations using both formal and informal social structures, it should prove useful when developing targeted awareness programmes that can be used to inform staff and students alike. Once these central individuals and locations have been identified, security awareness programmes using classic awareness items such as posters, pens, brochures, discussions, etc. can be used to inform people about security issues and thereby improve security awareness [23]. The purpose of the method proposed in this paper is therefore not to revolutionise traditional security awareness programmes, but merely to provide a way to improve their effectiveness and coverage in situations where security education and –training would not be feasible, and full-scale awareness programmes may be prohibitively expensive, or cause unwanted fatigue.

The remainder of this paper is organised as follows. In the next section, introductory background information with regards to some SNA metrics is provided. This is followed in Sect. 3 with the discussion of the proposed method, and two illustrative examples. A discussion of the findings is presented in Sect. 4, and in Sect. 5 the paper is concluded.

2 Background

2.1 Social Network Analysis

Any social organisation can be considered to be a series of interconnected networks, and as such standard graph modelling can be used to represent them. In such a network, nodes can be used to represent entities, such as people, knowledge, tasks or resources, whereas arcs can be used to represent the relationships that exist between them.

SNA allows for the quantitative analysis of a social organisation through graph theory, and various metrics can be calculated in order to analyse a network. Although a large number of metrics exists (a count of the work done by Clemente, Martins and Mendes [24] shows 28 metrics, whereas the help section of the ORA-Lite software suite names almost 200), only four basic metrics that are used in the illustrative examples will be briefly introduced. The discussion of the four SNA metrics is based on the work done in [21]. Comprehensive discussions of a large number of metrics can be found in a number of sources, such as [24–26].

Degree Centrality. The degree centrality measure is concerned with an individual node and more importantly the particular node's position within the network [21, 27]. A node's ability to influence a particular network is governed by its position within the network, and this in turn is referred to as the node's centrality measure [21]. There are a number of different types of centrality, but the core principle of centrality is that a node that is located more centrally, i.e. has more specific connection types than other nodes, will have a greater specific influence on the network as a whole. One of the quantitative measures used to describe the influence of such a node is referred to as its total degree centrality, and is calculated by using several node properties, such as the number of connections leading into the node, the number of connections leading out of the node, and the sum of the aforementioned connections [21]. A node with a high total degree centrality would be an excellent target for security awareness training, as any information injected into the network at this point is likely to propagate to the rest of the network in some way.

Closeness Centrality. Closeness centrality is calculated by determining all the geodesic distances (i.e. the shortest distances) to all other nodes within the network [21], and takes all indirect connections to other nodes that a node possesses, together with all direct connections, into account. A node that has a high closeness centrality value is considered to be a good source of information, whereas nodes with a high degree centrality value aids in the diffusion of information throughout the entire network. This means that analysis of the nodes with the greatest closeness centrality values should provide the best information with regard to the information in the network, and would therefore mitigate the need for full node-by-node network analysis.

Betweenness Centrality. When examining interactions between two non-adjacent nodes, the nodes that lie on the paths connecting the two nodes have some control over the interaction between the two nodes [28]. The betweenness centrality measure is a representation of the number of times that a particular node finds itself on the geodesic path of other nodes within the entire network [21]. This measure is reflective of the number of indirect nodes that are connected to a particular node. Thus, a node that has a high betweenness centrality measure would also be a good candidate to use to distribute knowledge and information throughout the network, as these types of node are exclusive, limited sources of information for parts of the network. There is, however, a downside to using such a node: a node with a high betweenness measure is at risk of being overburdened, as such a node would spend a portion, if not all, of its time facilitating interactions between other nodes.

A node that finds itself as an intermediary in an information exchange relationship between two nodes is also considered to be in a position of power, as any information exchanged between the two nodes has to go through the intermediary. The intermediary has a unique position of power in this instance, as it can determine not only the fidelity of the information being exchanged, but also whether information is exchanged at all. Thus, as the number of nodes that relies on such an intermediary increases, so too does the relative power the intermediary node possesses.

Eigenvector Centrality. Eigenvector centrality measures the extent to which a particular node is connected to other nodes that are considered to be highly connected or are of some particular importance [21]. Nodes that have a high eigenvector centrality value are important to note since they are considered to possess emergent leadership properties [29]. Nodes with a high eigenvector centrality are therefore also considered good targets for security awareness, as they tend to take on the roles of early adopters.

2.2 Network Formality

The formality of a network within the context of this paper is a measure of how formal the relationships that are used to construct a social network are. A highly formal network will utilize formal relationships, such as reporting structures, while a less formal network will make use of what is known as informal information systems (IIS). These systems are of particular interest, as they are found in every organisation and present one of the many places where SNA can be applied. IIS are special types of information system that represent the so-called "grapevine" of an organisation [30]. IIS are characterised by their lack of formal structure, their questionable reliability and their possible incompatibility with formal information systems. Unfortunately, due to their ability to collect a significantly greater subset of data, IIS are often crucial to business processes [31, 32]. It is important to take note of these types of information system, as they can have a profound impact on the flow of information within an organisation and must therefore be considered when developing a method that relies on the characteristics of a social network to improve security awareness within an organisation. Depending on the organisation, it may be necessary to target the social networks associated with IIS, rather than those networks associated with its formal structures, in order to obtain the desired results with regards to information security awareness. In an academic environment, for example, it is important to target both the more formal networks that include relationships, such as reporting structures and teaching responsibilities, and the less formal networks, such as those that include social relationships between students.

3 Method

The methodology employed in this paper broadly follows the DPA-method, with a number of notable exceptions:

- The DPA-method uses formal networks constructed from an organisation's hierarchy, whereas the method proposed here targets both formal and informal social networks;
- The method proposed in this study specifically targets personnel and students in an academic setup, such as a university, rather than an organisation; and
- The information security awareness programmes developed using the method in this study can be used to structure a programme that ideally targets the expected awareness level of a group, whereas in the DPA-method a number of influential employees are fully trained in information security awareness.

The proposed method is executed in three primary phases: Preparation, Network Construction, and Evaluation and Implementation. The basic process of the method is shown in Fig. 1.

The first phase, namely the **Preparation** phase, focusses on developing a clear and congruent approach to implementing the method. During this phase, a number of issues crucial to obtaining useful SNA data are addressed. The first of these issues deals with properly "bordering" the group the awareness programme is to target. In an academic environment, bordering may include aspects, such as field of study, the faculty they belong to, their lecturers, etc. This phase also focusses on determining the scope and formality of the networks that will be used.

The **Network Construction** phase is primarily focussed on collecting and processing the network data needed to identify the target individuals. This phase focuses on selecting data collection methods that can be used to construct social networks. These methods may include questionnaires, email-scanning, class-list processing, etc. if a more informal network was selected. Otherwise, formal organisational structures, such as reporting hierarchies can be used, which negate the necessity of using intrusive techniques, such as questionnaires and email-scanning. Once the members of the group have been identified and the nature of the relationships between them has been established, the social network can be constructed. This, along with the calculation of the metrics, is ideally done using software. In this phase, the impact of selecting a more formal or a less formal network will also become clear. Should the impact of the network formality be too great in a negative sense, the Preparation phase should be repeated in order to either negate or mitigate the impact.

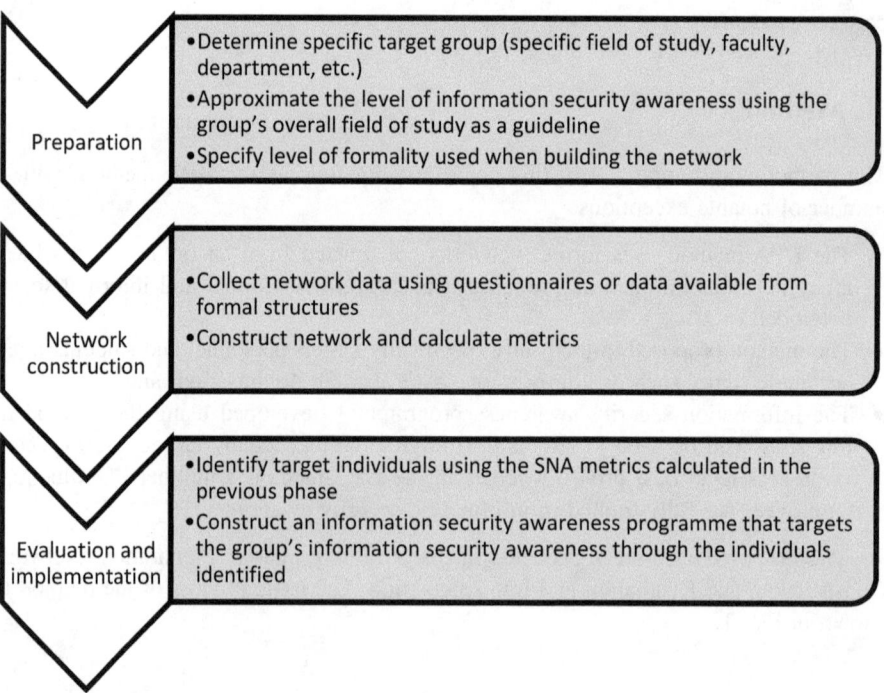

Fig. 1. Process of the proposed method, showing progression through the three phases

During the final **Evaluation and Implementation** phase, the data from the previous two phases are used to determine both the contents of the awareness programme and its intended targets. The specifics of the awareness programme's contents will likely differ from case to case, as the programme should be adapted to the targeted individual, as well as the group in general.

3.1 Illustrative Examples

To illustrate the feasibility of the proposed approach, two practical experiments were conducted. In the first experiment an informal social network construction approach was used, whereas a formal social network was utilised in the second experiment.

Case Study 1. During the Preparation phase a target group of 25 post-graduate students was chosen. An informal social network construction approach was decided upon, as there were no significant formal connections amongst the students apart from attending the same class. In the Network construction phase data were obtained from the students. The following social question was posed to the students:

> *Suppose the computer security group is invited to a function by the industry and everyone shows up. The venue is properly decorated and a number of round tables have been prepared, with exactly one chair for each of the students. If you could make the decision, who would you prefer to have on your right- and left-hand side at the table?*

The response rate was 68%, which was deemed adequate for demonstration purposes.

Respondents were given the option of choosing from a list of names that correspond to the students registered for the class. The data obtained were analysed using ORA-Lite [33], which was also used to construct the network. The four measures discussed in Sect. 2 were calculated and are used in the next phase to determine candidates for disseminating security awareness information through the network. The network obtained is presented in Fig. 2.

During the final Evaluation and Implementation phase, the calculated measures were evaluated to identify candidates that should be targeted. Results indicated that node LR has the highest betweenness centrality at 0.028, eigenvector centrality at 0.322, and total-degree centrality at 0.174, while node CP has the highest closeness centrality at 0.055. These values indicate that the best singular candidate to target would be node LR. An evaluation of the network shown in Fig. 2, however, shows that selecting only node LR will not be entirely effective as there are three distinct, unconnected networks. Therefore, in order to expose the entire network, nodes AG, which is visually the centre of subnetwork B, and node LS in subnetwork C, which has a betweenness centrality of 0.01, an eigenvector centrality of 0.156, and a total-degree centrality of 0.109, should also be targeted.

Case Study 2. For Case Study 2 a formal network construction approach was chosen. The relationships between the personnel at a Computer Science department at a South African university and their formal post-graduate students were used. Where duplicate connections were found, for instance where one student received guidance from more than one member of the department, the weight of the existing connection was increased to indicate a closer relationship. The same three phases used in Case Study 1 were used and the network shown in Fig. 3 was obtained. The data were anonymised, and the node names were chosen to differentiate between students and staff. All node names that contain a D represent staff and all nodes that contain an N represent students. From Fig. 3 as well as the metrics calculated from this network, it is clear that nodes D60, D49, D14 and D76 represent the most connected and influential members in this network. Node D60 in particular has the highest value in all four metrics, which indicates that this person is not only an emergent leader within the network, but is also an influencer. This makes sense as this node is a member of the academic staff who has a large number of students that also receives guidance from other members of staff. Node D76 is also a good target as the node has the second-highest total-degree centrality value. The node does, however, have a significantly lower eigenvector centrality value, and the reduced leadership influence may impact the efficacy of using this node as a target. The ideal situation would involve all four of these individuals, namely D60, D49, D14 and D76, being targeted in information security awareness programmes. As these four individuals are likely to have regular meetings or discussions, any information passed to them should disseminate through the network relatively quickly and naturally.

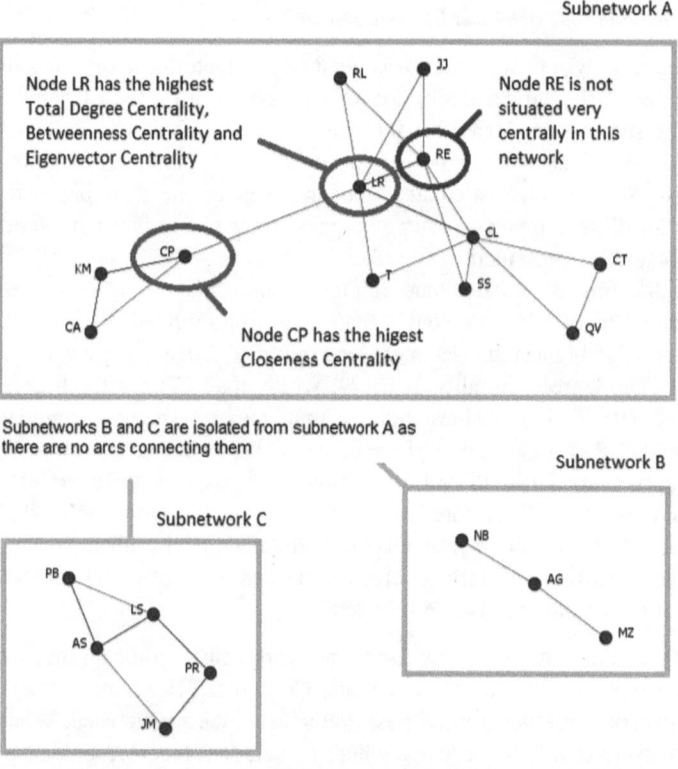

Fig. 2. Social network based on the informal social question

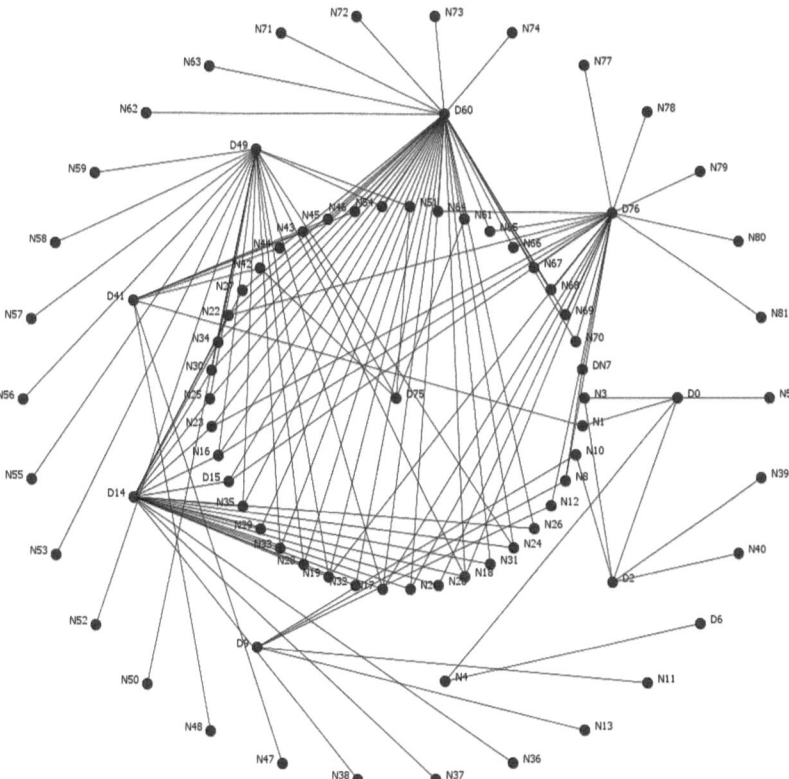

Fig. 3. Formal network of the computer science lecturers and post-graduate students

4 Discussion

The organisational structure of universities generally differs from more traditional organisations in that an academic organisation incorporates a large number of students, which are generally not part of a formal management structure. Universities also differ from other organisational structures in that the various departments at a university are quite often isolated from one another. While it is likely that an administration department may have contact with all the various faculties, it is generally quite rare for separate faculties to have frequent contact with one another. These aspects of an academic organisation make it difficult to target both the staff and the students at a university. While possible in theory, in practice it is difficult to provide information security training to both students and staff, as there is no simple way to organise events of such a size. In addition to the logistical difficulties, neither students nor staff like attending awareness training sessions, especially if there is a perception that no new information will be provided. These problems are further compounded by the financial limitations most universities have to implement in order to remain solvent. Security awareness training for a whole university will likely require significant funds. Such an investment, as far as most universities are concerned, offers too little in return.

The two case studies presented in this paper demonstrate that SNA is a feasible alternative to large scale security awareness programmes in an academic environment, due to a number of reasons. The first of these reasons is that both formal and informal techniques and relationships can be used to construct social networks, which means that there is no absolute dependency on specific structures. This is an advantage in academic environments where a comprehensive formal structure may be limited or non-existent. Another reason is that a handful of individuals can be identified for targeted awareness training. This significantly reduces the cost and, as the topics of the awareness programmes can be selected to correspond to the individual's level of information security knowledge, the chances of fatigue are also drastically reduced. A further advantage is that security awareness can be addressed less formally and more consistently: as new threats are identified, the various targeted individuals can be informed with minimal cost and effort. These individuals will also have a known level of information security knowledge, which will make a continuous programme more effective. SNA is also a relatively simple method to implement, as software packages that implement it do not require overly complex data in order to produce results. This makes the technique relatively easy to implement and use. A final advantage is that any number of networks can be constructed concurrently in order to target a large group. If say, for example, two departments have no contact with one another and their internal organisational structures are too distinct, a network can be constructed for each department using bordering techniques that are appropriate to each department.

5   Conclusion

Information security awareness programmes have to be implemented and used with great care in order to be effective. In more traditional organisations, formal awareness programmes are generally used to address information security awareness shortcomings. In academic organisations, where formal structures do not necessarily include all the members of the organisation, such as students, it is often much more difficult to conduct effective security awareness training. In this paper, in an attempt to address some of the problems of conducting security awareness training in an academic environment, the feasibility of using SNA to develop targeted awareness programmes was investigated. Two illustrative examples, one using formal structures and the other informal relationships, were presented to demonstrate that SNA is a feasible alternative to formal awareness programmes in an academic environment.

The contribution of this study is that the suggested approach, that may be easier and faster to use, and reduce certain limitations, such as costs, fatigue, and the inclusion of information that is inappropriate for the target audience, is indeed feasible. Future work will include the use of more extensive tests, such as the use of larger sample groups and the monitoring of information security levels, to demonstrate the usability of the presented method. These studies will also show how effective, both in terms of cost and coverage, the proposed method is when compared to untargeted, traditional awareness programmes.

References

1. Shillair, R., Cotten, S.R., Tsai, H.S., Alhabash, S., LaRose, R., Rifon, N.J.: Online safety begins with you and me: convincing Internet users to protect themselves. Comput. Hum. Behav. **48**, 199–207 (2015)
2. Parsons, K., McCormac, A., Butavicius, M., Pattinson, M., Jerram, C.: Determining employee awareness using the Human Aspects of Information Security Questionnaire (HAIS-Q). Comput. Secur. **42**, 165–176 (2014)
3. Soomro, Z.A., Shah, M.H., Ahmed, J.: Information security management needs more holistic approach: a literature review. Int. J. Inf. Manage. **36**(2), 215–225 (2016)
4. Rezgui, Y., Marks, A.: Information security awareness in higher education: an exploratory study. Comput. Secur. **27**(7–8), 241–253 (2008). https://doi.org/10.1016/j.cose.2008.07.008
5. Byrne, Z.S., Dvorak, K.J., Peters, J.M., Ray, I., Howe, A., Sanchez, D.: From the user's perspective: perceptions of risk relative to benefit associated with using the internet. Comput. Hum. Behav. **59**, 456–468 (2016)
6. Arachchilage, N.A.G., Love, S.: Security awareness of computer users: a phishing threat avoidance perspective. Comput. Hum. Behav. **38**, 304–312 (2014)
7. Aloul, F.A.: The need for effective information security awareness. J. Adv. Inf. Technol. **3**(3), 176–183 (2012)
8. Chen, C.C., Medlin, B.D., Shaw, R.S.: A cross-cultural investigation of situational information security awareness programs. Inf. Manage. Comput. Secur. **16**(4), 360–376 (2008)
9. Thomson, M.E., von Solms, R.: Information security awareness: educating your users effectively. Inf. Manage. Comput. Secur. **6**(4), 167–173 (1998)
10. Siponen, M.T.: A conceptual foundation for organizational information security awareness. Inf. Manage. Comput. Secur. **8**(1), 31–41 (2000)
11. Kruger, H.A., Kearney, W.D.: A prototype for assessing information security awareness. Comput. Secur. **25**(4), 289–296 (2006)
12. Ng, B., Kankanhalli, A., Xu, Y.: Studying users' computer security behavior: a health belief perspective. Decis. Support Syst. **46**(4), 815–825 (2009)
13. Tsohou, A., Karyda, M., Kokolakis, S.: Analysing the role of cognitive and cultural biases in the internalization of information security policies: recommendations for information security awareness programs. Comput. Secur. **52**, 128–141 (2015)
14. Boksem, M.A.S., Tops, M.: Mental fatigue: costs and benefits. Brain Res. Rev. **59**(1), 125–139 (2008). https://doi.org/10.1016/j.brainresrev.2008.07.001
15. van der Linden, D., Frese, M., Meijman, T.F.: Mental fatigue and the control of cognitive processes: effects on perseveration and planning. Acta Psychol. **113**(1), 45–65 (2003). https://doi.org/10.1016/S0001-6918(02)00150-6
16. Furnell, S., Thomson, K.-L.: Recognising and addressing 'security fatigue'. Comput. Fraud Secur. **2009**(11), 7–11 (2009). https://doi.org/10.1016/S1361-3723(09)70139-3
17. Scott, J., Carrington, P.J.: The SAGE Handbook of Social Network Analysis, SAGE Publications (2011)
18. Fu, J., Sun, D., Chai, J., Xiao, J., Wang, S.: The "six-element" analysis method for the research on the characteristics of terrorist activities. Ann. Oper. Res. **234**, 17–35 (2015)
19. Philips, E., Nurse, J., Goldsmith, M., Creese, S.: Applying social network analysis to security. In: Working Papers of the Sustainable Society Network, pp. 11–27 (2015)
20. Dang-Pham, D., Pittayachawan, S., Bruno, V.: Applications of social network analysis in behavioural information security research: concepts and empirical analysis. Comput. Secur. **68**, 1–15 (2017)

21. Armstrong, H.L., McCulloh, I.: Organizational risk using network analysis. In: Proceedings of South African Information Security Multi-Conference (2010)
22. Armstrong, H., Armstrong, C., McCulloh, I.: A Course Applying Network Analysis to Organizational Risk in Information Security (2010)
23. Whitman, M.E., Mattord, H.J.: Principles of Information Security. Cengage Learning (2011)
24. Clemente, F.M., Martins, F.M.L., Mendes, R.S.: Social network analysis applied to team sports analysis. SAST. Springer, Cham (2016). https://doi.org/10.1007/978-3-319-25855-3
25. Brin, S., Page, L.: The anatomy of a large-scale hypertextual web search engine. Comput. Netw. ISDN Syst. **30**(1–7), 107–117 (1998)
26. Freeman, L.C., Roeder, D., Mulholland, R.R.: Centrality in social networks: II. Experimental results. Soc. Netw. **2**(2), 119–141 (1979)
27. Hanneman, R.A., Riddle, M.: Introduction to Social Network Methods. University of California (2005)
28. Wasserman, S., Faust, K.: Social Network Analysis: Methods and Applications. Cambridge University Press, Cambridge (1994)
29. Borgatti, S.P.: Centrality and network flow. Soc. Netw. **27**, 55–71 (2005)
30. Clancy, D.K., Collins, F.: Informal accounting information systems: some tentative findings. Account. Organ. Soc. **4**(1–2), 21–30 (1979)
31. MacDonald, S.: Informal information flow and strategy in the international firm. Int. J. Technol. Manage. **11**(1–2), 219–232 (1996)
32. Duncombe, R., Heeks, R.: Enterprise across the digital divide: information systems and rural microenterprise in Botswana. J. Int. Dev. **14**(1), 61–74 (2002)
33. CASOS, "ORA-Lite" (2018). www.casos.cs.cmu.edu/projects/ora

Factors Influencing Smartphone Application Downloads

Wiehan Janse Van Rensburg(ID), Kerry-Lynn Thomson(✉)(ID),
and Lynn Futcher(ID)

Nelson Mandela University, Port Elizabeth, South Africa
{s213461846,kerry-lynn.thomson,
lynn.futcher}@mandela.ac.za

Abstract. Mobile applications are increasingly being downloaded in modern society. Despite providing many benefits to potential users, many such applications pose security risks to their users including the leaking of personal information. When applications provide features that fulfil the users' needs, smartphone users often neglect to consider security when downloading applications. This paper explores whether students consider relevant Security Factors when selecting an application to download. A Smartphone Simulation Exercise and related questions were used to determine students' reported behaviour regarding smartphone application downloads. The findings suggest that many students do not consider relevant Security Factors important when downloading applications and, therefore, need to be educated in this regard.

Keywords: Mobile applications · Smartphone behaviour
Secure application downloads · Security Factors

1 Introduction

The number of global smartphone users has grown significantly over the past years, and it is estimated that by the end of 2018, there will be 2.53 billion smartphone users globally [1]. With this demand for smartphones, the need for mobile applications has also increased. The most widely adopted operating system (OS) amongst smartphone users is Android OS having more than 80% of the market share [2]. Smartphone users can choose from millions of applications found in application marketplaces, such as Google Play Store, and it is estimated that smartphone users spend 90% of their time on mobile applications [3]. Smartphone users who download applications are generally aware of the benefits that the applications can provide but are often not aware of the associated risks that these applications can pose [4].

As smartphones become omnipresent in society, increased amounts of private information regarding smartphone users are being collected and shared by the applications they use. Further, due to the distribution models employed, application marketplaces have become targets of cybercrime, making it easy for attackers to upload malicious applications. Smartphone users that download applications but neglect to review the security of the application could find themselves using malicious applications that could have a negative impact on their privacy and personal information.

L. Drevin and M. Theocharidou (Eds.): WISE 2018, IFIP AICT 531, pp. 81–92, 2018.
https://doi.org/10.1007/978-3-319-99734-6_7

Therefore, security should be considered by smartphone users when downloading applications.

This paper highlights eight factors that should be considered by smartphone users when downloading an application. The eight factors identified were based on what the Google Play Policy stipulates should be contained within the application listing and on what smartphone users typically see when viewing applications listed within the Google Play Store. The Google Play Developer Policy Center specifies to the developers what they should consider whilst developing an application and this forms the guidelines as to what developers should adhere to [5]. However, only those aspects that are visible to the user when downloading an application were used for this study. The eight factors identified are Application Rating, Application Reviews, Number of Downloads, Detailed Information, Privacy Policy, Permissions Requested, the Developer of the Application, and when the Last Update was released.

The purpose of this paper is to identify whether Information Technology students from a typical higher educational institution in South Africa consider relevant security factors when selecting an application to download. This research focused on the reported behaviour of the students regarding application downloads. A Smartphone Simulation Exercise to determine students' reported behaviour was conducted to identify the most influential factors that students consider when selecting an application to download. The use of simulations allows students to engage within real world situations. This form of teaching also includes group discussions, debates, collaborative projects and internships. This can include any method that asks students to help develop and apply their knowledge [6]. The use of simulations can recreate complex processes in the classroom, allowing students to examine the motivations, behavioural constraints, resources and interactions amongst institutional actors [7]. In this context, students can immerse themselves in real decision-making processes, and thus allowing the course content to become more relevant.

This was followed by related questions regarding their general smartphone usage and general security awareness relating to smartphone application downloads.

The structure of the paper is as follows: Sect. 2 provides background on smartphone usage and related threats, while Sect. 3 presents the eight factors which were used in the study. Section 4 discusses the research process followed and the results and findings of the study are presented in Sect. 5, with a related discussion in Sect. 6. Section 7 concludes the paper.

2 Smartphone Usage

The adoption of smartphones amongst users has seen a significant increase because of the wide variety of productivity tools, entertainment, functions, and special features offered through their associated applications [8].

Most smartphone users download and install applications, but neglect to review the privacy policies of the applications [9]. These applications, once granted the permissions, have the ability to collect, store, and transmit the personal and private information they collect. Smartphone users often unknowingly surrender personal information for the expected benefits that smartphone applications might provide, but the release of private information might also come with related risk. Smartphone users that download applications, but do not take security into consideration, could unknowingly authorize access to some protected resources or allow an application to alter users' privacy and security settings due to a lack of awareness regarding the risk posed by applications.

Information security on a smartphone can be seen as the knowledge, attitude, and behaviour that users apply in protecting their personal information [4]. The different types of information that can be found on smartphone devices includes; personal, organizational, financial, authentication, connectivity, or service information [10]. Traditionally, information security was focused on addressing technical solutions to secure users' information assets stored on their devices and little focus was placed on users and their responsibilities. Smartphone users need to take control with regards to information security [11]. The next section presents eight factors, identified through literature that influence smartphone application downloads.

3   Typical Factors Within Application Listings

When application developers design and develop applications to upload onto the Google Play Store, they are required to adhere to the relevant policies regarding what should be included within an application listing. Google Play's Developer Policy Center outlines to developers what is required when listing an application on the Play Store to help encourage users to download their application. Within this policy it includes aspects such as App Promotions, Metadata, User Ratings, Reviews, Installs, and Content Ratings [5]. When smartphone users download applications, they would generally look at what information the application listing contains and base their decision to download an application on the information provided. Within an application listing, the following eight factors, as shown in Table 1, can be used to gather more information about an application.

From the eight factors identified in Table 1, four factors can be seen as General Factors to consider when selecting an application. The General Factors include Application Rating, Application Reviews, Number of Downloads and Detailed Information. The remaining four factors relate directly to security and are therefore referred to as Security Factors in this paper. As security should be a concern when smartphone users download applications, the four Security Factors of Privacy Policy, Permissions Requested, Last Update Released of the application, and the Developer Information of the application should be key considerations when selecting an application to download. This paper details how important the Information Technology students considered Security Factors throughout the process of downloading an application. The next section presents the research process of the study.

Table 1. Typical factors within an application listing.

Factors	Description of factors
Application rating	The application rating can be seen as a measure to define whether the application has value. Google Play uses a five-star rating scale for users to express their experience with the application. Users associate a high rating with a good application and a low rating as bad. This factor is not security related, but more an indication on how the users experienced the application
Application reviews	The application review is provided by users of the application. Within the reviews, users express the common problems they are experiencing with the application, as well as highlighting their good experiences. Reading reviews is a good way for potential users to see how others feel about the application. Users depend on reviews to assist them when selecting an application to download. This factor relates to user satisfaction
Number of downloads	The number of downloads is typically linked to the popularity of the application. Applications with a high number of downloads are widely used. However, this does not necessarily indicate whether the application is secure
Detailed information	This section usually highlights the features of the application as well as providing screenshots of the user interface, but rarely includes security related information. The detailed information typically includes information about the developer and when last the application was updated
Privacy policy	If the application is collecting, storing, or sharing personal information, an application generally discloses this within the privacy policy. It is important from a security point of view for users to review the privacy policy of an application, as it can indicate how the application intends to use any information it collects
Permissions requested	The permissions requested by the application is what is required to ensure the full functionality of the application once downloaded. However, there are applications that request access to more information than what the application needs to function. This could violate the privacy of smartphone users' information
Last update released	Applications need to be updated to enhance the application functions, performance, stability, and security. Frequently updated applications can be a good indication of whether the application is still being supported by its developer. Outdated applications could potentially contain vulnerabilities which can be exploited
Developer information	Typical information that can be found regarding the developer includes their full name, list of their published applications, and contact details. This would indicate whether the application is from the original developer. Downloading an application from a non-reputable developer could result in the download of a malicious application

4   Research Process

This research focused on the reported behaviour of first year IT students. The study was conducted by firstly performing a Smartphone Simulation Exercise, followed by related questions. The sample of students was selected based on convenience as the researcher had access to the sample of students whose curriculum included smartphone behaviour as part of their IT skills course.

The Smartphone Simulation Exercise was conducted in controlled computer labs and students were given two scenarios and asked to download one application per scenario. In the first scenario seen in Fig. 1, the students were given a list of six Photo Editing Applications, while in the second scenario seen in Fig. 2, students were given a list of five Alarm Clock applications from which to choose.

Fig. 1. First scenario applications

Fig. 2. Second scenario applications

Once the students completed the Smartphone Simulation Exercise, related questions were presented to the students.

The students were given eight questions directly linked to the eight factors discussed in Table 1. Each question asked, 'Did you consider the (*factor*) when selecting the application to download?'. For each of the questions, four options were given:

- Yes, but only for the application I downloaded.
- Yes, but only for a few of the applications listed.
- Yes, I considered the (*factor*) for all the applications listed.
- No, I did not consider the (*factor*).

Further questions were used to identify students' smartphone awareness related to smartphone application downloads, and their smartphone adoption, usage, knowledge, perceptions and privacy concerns. This paper, however, primarily reports back on factors related to the decision-making processes during the application download in the Smartphone Simulation Exercises.

Participating students were from various demographic backgrounds and all Smartphone Simulation Exercises and related questions that were successfully completed were taken into consideration. The following section presents the results and findings from the study.

5   Results and Findings

Although 228 students participated in the Smartphone Simulation Exercise, only 224 responses were considered valid due to incomplete questions. These questions covered the consideration of students with regards to the General Factors and Security Factors when selecting an application to download. When asked how long it took them to decide which application to download, 64% of students took less than 5 min to select an application in each scenario.

After the students completed the Smartphone Simulation Exercise and its accompanying questions, the students were presented with a further question which related to their general awareness with regards to security considerations when downloading an application. The results from the study conducted indicated that the students spend, on average, more than 4 h a day on their smartphones. The students download applications and spend most of their time on the internet, listening to music and being actively involved on social media. The most popular social media platforms amongst these students were WhatsApp, YouTube, Facebook, and Instagram. Smartphones are used for various purposes and personal information is stored on the devices. Over 75% of students stated that they would be extremely concerned if their personal information stored on their smartphone was lost or stolen.

The following sub-sections present the results from the Smartphone Simulation Exercise and the related questions.

5.1   General Factors

As can be seen in Table 2, when selecting an application to download, the students consider the General Factors of Application Reviews, Application Rating, Number of Downloads, and Detailed Information as important in their decision-making process. As can be seen in Table 2, 89.7% of students considered the Application Reviews for one or more applications listed in the scenarios, 93.3% considered the Application Rating for one or more applications listed in the scenarios, 74% took the Number of Downloads of the application into consideration when selecting an application for download, and 79.7% read the Detailed Information of the application for one or more applications listed in the scenarios.

5.2   Security Factors

As can be seen in Table, 3, when selecting an application to download, the students do not consider the Security Factors of Privacy Policy, Last Update, Permissions

Table 2. General factors when downloading

Options	App reviews	App rating	Number of downloads	Detailed info
Yes, I considered the *factor* for one or more applications	**89.7%**	**93.3%**	**74.0%**	**79.7%**
– Yes, but only for the one I downloaded	22.3%	16.5%	21.0%	33.2%
– Yes, but only for a few of the applications listed	29.9%	17.0%	20.0%	25.7%
– Yes, I considered the *factor* for all applications listed	37.5%	59.8%	33.0%	20.8%
No, I did not consider the *Factor*	**10.3%**	**6.7%**	**26.0%**	**20.3%**

Requested, and Developer Information as important as the General Factors. The majority of students stated that they did not consider the Security Factors during the process of selecting an application to download. As can be seen in Table 3, 58.5% of students did not review the Privacy Policy of the application when deciding which application to download, 56% indicated that they did not consider the Last Update released for the application, 38.6% did not review the Permissions Requested when selecting an application to download, and 63.4% indicated that they did not consider the Developer Information.

Table 3. Security factors when downloading

Options	Privacy policy	Last update	Permissions requested	Developer info
Yes, I considered the *factor* for one or more applications	**41.5%**	**44.0%**	**61.4%**	**36.6%**
– Yes, but only for the one I downloaded	19.6%	22.8%	36.4%	19.5%
– Yes, but only for a few of the applications listed	9.4%	11.4%	12.5%	10.0%
– Yes, I considered the *factor* for all applications listed	12.5%	9.8%	12.5%	7.1%
No, I did not consider the *Factor*	**58.5%**	**56.0%**	**38.6%**	**63.4%**

Based on these results, the General Factors and Security Factors were ranked to indicate what students considered important when downloading an application. Table 4 ranks the factors based on the percentage of students that considered these factors important. In the table it is clearly shown that a lot more consideration was given to the General Factors and less consideration was placed on the Security Factors.

Table 4. Student consideration ranking

	Students consideration when selecting an application	% of students that considered the factor
General factors	1. Application rating	93.3%
	2. Application reviews	89.7%
	3. Detailed information	79.7%
	4. Number of downloads	74.0%
Security factors	5. Permissions requested	61.4%
	6. Last update	44.0%
	7. Privacy policy	41.5%
	8. Developer information	36.6%

The factors identified in Table 4 relate to the eight factors in Table 1 and were based on students' reported behaviour on how they selected the applications they downloaded. A further question determined students' general security awareness regarding the secure downloading of applications.

This question was not related to the Smartphone Simulation Exercise, but asked which General Factors and Security Factors students considered important from a security point of view when selecting an application to download. This question was a general perception question that related to security and asked students to rank the importance of given factors from highest to lowest. The factors given to students were App Rating, App Reviews, Privacy Policy, App Permissions, and Developer Information. General Factors were added to the list of factors to determine if students could make a distinction between General Factors and Security Factors. The results from this question were used to determine whether students consider relevant Security Factors as important when selecting an application.

Table 5 shows an example of how the Cumulative Importance Value is calculated for Privacy Policy. The values in the table are calculated based on the importance ranking (X) multiplied by the number of students who ranked that specific factor (Y). The importance ranking consisted of six levels of importance, ranging from Most Important (6), Very Important (5), Fairly Important (4), Important (3), Less Important (2), and Least Important (1). Each student could only assign an importance ranking once to a factor. All Calculated Importance Values for each factor were added together to provide the final Cumulative Importance Value.

Table 6 ranks the importance value of each factor from highest to lowest according to how students indicated the importance of each factor from a security point of view.

From the factors provided in this question, two related to the General Factors of Application Rating and Application Reviews, while three related to the Security Factors of Privacy Policy, Permissions Requested and Developer Information. The results in Table 6 show that Privacy Policy is the most important factor students would consider when selecting an application. Further, students incorrectly perceived General Factors as security related as two from the top three factors were General Factors. These two factors, however, do not have any impact on the security of an application. As Privacy Policy was identified as the top security related factor followed by General

Table 5. Example of cumulative importance value calculation for privacy policy

	Importance ranking (X)	Number of times (factor) ranked (Y)	Calculation (X × Y)	Calculated importance value
Factor	6	67	6 × 67	402
(Privacy	5	43	5 × 43	215
policy)	4	38	4 × 38	152
	3	35	3 × 35	105
	2	16	2 × 16	32
	1	10	1 × 10	10
Cumulative importance value				**916**

Table 6. Importance value

Factors	Cumulative importance value
Privacy policy	916
App rating	768
App reviews	736
App permission	718
Developer information	695

Factors it is apparent that students cannot make a clear distinction between General Factors and Security Factors.

6 Towards an Educational Intervention

The Smartphone Simulation Exercise was set up to determine students' reported behaviour when selecting an application to download and students were asked to complete the Smartphone Simulation Exercise followed by related questions. These questions identify students' decision-making process throughout the process of selecting an application by determining what General Factors and Security Factors they considered when downloading an application. The results of the study show that students tend to consider General Factors in the application listing as more important than Security Factors when downloading an application.

Thereafter, an additional question not related to the Smartphone Simulation Exercise was asked to identify students' general perception related to security when downloading an application. The additional question asked which factors are perceived important when considering security during the selection of an application. The results of this question shows that students perceive factors such as Application Rating and Application Reviews as security related while they are, in fact, are General factors. Furthermore students stated that considering the Privacy Policy of an application is the most important factor related to security, and more than 75% of students stated that they would be extremely concerned if their privacy was compromised when downloading an application. However, this was not reflected in their reported behaviour in the Smartphone Simulation Exercise, as only 41.5% of the students considered the Privacy Policy when selecting an application to download.

Security Factors should be important considerations when downloading a smartphone application. However, the majority of students participating in the study (58.5%) did not deem the Security Factors important in the Smartphone Simulation Exercise. Therefore, it can be argued that an educational intervention is needed to make students aware of the potential risks associated with not considering Security Factors.

Table 7 below shows the Security Factors that should be addressed through an educational intervention.

Table 7. Security factors to be addressed through an educational intervention

Security factor	What must be addressed
Permissions requested	It is important that users read the Permissions Requested carefully to ensure the application is not requesting access to unnecessary information
	If Permissions Requested are not considered, it could have a negative impact on their privacy and personal information
	For example, an Alarm Clock Application should not need access to user contact details, e-mails, and photos
Last update	It is important that users check when last the application was updated to ensure it is still supported by its developers
	If the Last Update is not considered, the application could be outdated and unsupported, and may not have the necessary security patches and updates. An unsupported application could be vulnerable to malicious attacks and an easy target for cybercriminals to exploit
Privacy policy	It is important that users read the Privacy Policy of an application before downloading to determine if the application will be collecting, storing or sharing personal information collected
	If the Privacy Policy is not considered, personal information could unknowingly be disclosed to third-parties
	For example, WhatsApp has been certified to the EU-U.S. Privacy Shield Framework and the Swiss-U.S. Privacy Shield Framework regarding the collection and processing of personal data of business partners [12]
Developer information	It is important that users review the Developer Information to ensure that the application is from the original developer and not a cloned version of the application, which may include malware. Popular applications are often cloned and made freely available to entice users to download the application
	For example, Rovio Entertainment Corporation is the original developer of the popular 'Angry Birds' application. However, a fake version of 'Angry Birds Space' contained malware which downloads additional malware to the smartphone and enlists the smartphone as part of a botnet [13]

Future research will develop an educational intervention that will address each of these Security Factors, the related risks and how they could be mitigated in order to increase students' security awareness when downloading an application. This educational intervention will be presented to the same sample of students, followed by a further set of questions to determine any changes in their level of security awareness when downloading smartphone applications.

7 Conclusion

Being aware of Security Factors when downloading a smartphone application can help reduce the risk of potentially downloading a malicious application. The study determined the students' reported behaviour with regards to their process of selecting an application to download. Over 75% of students indicated that they were concerned about the privacy of their personal information, however this was not reflected in their reported behaviour. An educational intervention could create awareness amongst students and educate them on the factors that should be considered when selecting an application to download.

Acknowledgements. The financial assistance of the National Research Foundation (NRF) towards this research is hereby acknowledged. Opinions expressed, and conclusions arrived at, are those of the authors, and cannot necessarily be attributed to the NRF.

References

1. Statista, Smartphone users worldwide 2014–2020. https://www.statista.com/statistics/330695/number-of-smartphone-users-worldwide/. Accessed 15 Apr 2018
2. Statista, Share of global population that uses a smartphone 2014–2021. https://www.statista.com/statistics/203734/global-smartphone-penetration-per-capita-since-2005/. Accessed 15 Apr 2018
3. Chaffey, D.: Percent time spent on mobile apps (2016). http://www.smartinsights.com/mobile-marketing/mobile-marketing-analytics/mobile-marketing-statistics/attachment/percent-time-spent-on-mobile-apps-2016/. Accessed 8 Aug 2017
4. Allam, S., Flowerday, S.V., Flowerday, E.: Smartphone information security awareness: a victim of operational pressures. Comput. Secur. 42, 56–65 (2014). https://doi.org/10.1016/j.cose.2014.01.005
5. Google Play, Developer Policy Center. https://play.google.com/about/developer-content-policy-print/. Accessed 18 Apr 2018
6. Shaw, C.M.: Designing and using simulations and role-play exercises. The International Studies Encyclopedia. Robert A. Blackwell Publishing, Denmark (2010)
7. Smith, E.T., Boyer, M.A.: Designing in-class simulations. Polit. Sci. Polit. **29**(6), 690–694 (1997)
8. Awad, N., Krishnan, M.: The personalization privacy paradox: an empirical evaluation of information transparency and the willingness to be profiled online for personalization. MIS Q. **30**(1), 13–28 (2006). https://doi.org/10.2307/25148715

9. Negash, S., Shahriar, H.: Mobile app permissions awareness. In: 2015 5th International Conference on Information & Communication Technology and Accessibility (ICTA), pp. 1–4. IEEE (2015)
10. Theoharidou, M., Mylonas, A., Gritzalis, D.: A risk assessment method for smartphones. In: Gritzalis, D., Furnell, S., Theoharidou, M. (eds.) SEC 2012. IAICT, vol. 376, pp. 443–456. Springer, Heidelberg (2012). https://doi.org/10.1007/978-3-642-30436-1_36
11. Furnell, S., Clarke, N.: Power to the people? The evolving recognition of human aspects of security. Comput. Secur. **31**(8), 983–988 (2012)
12. Privacy Shield Framework, WhatsApp Inc. https://www.privacyshield.gov/participant?id=a2zt0000000TSnwAAG. Accessed 30 Jun 2018
13. Cluley, G.: Android malware poses as Angry Bird Space game (2012). https://nakedsecurity.sophos.com/2012/04/12/android-malware-angry-birds-space-game/. Accessed 30 Jun 2018

Information Security Courses and Curricula

A MOOC on Privacy by Design and the GDPR

Simone Fischer-Hübner[1], Leonardo A. Martucci[1(✉)], Lothar Fritsch[1],
Tobias Pulls[1], Sebastian Herold[1], Leonardo H. Iwaya[1], Stefan Alfredsson[1],
and Albin Zuccato[2]

[1] Karlstad University, Karlstad, Sweden
{simone.fischer-huebner,leonardo.martucci,lothar.fritsch,tobias.pulls,
sebastian.herold,leonardo.iwaya,stefan.alfredsson}@kau.se
[2] ATEA Sverige AB, Stockholm, Sweden
albin.zuccato@atea.se

Abstract. In this paper we describe how we designed a massive open online course (MOOC) on Privacy by Design with a focus on how to achieve compliance with the EU GDPR principles and requirements in IT engineering and management. This MOOC aims at educating both professionals and undergraduate students, i.e., target groups with distinct educational needs and requirements, within a single course structure. We discuss why developing and publishing such a course is a timely decision and fulfills the current needs of the professional and undergraduate education. The MOOC is organized in five modules, each of them with its own learning outcomes and activities. The modules focus on different aspects of the GDPR that data protection officers have to be knowledgeable about, ranging from the legal basics, to data protection impact assessment methods, and privacy-enhancing technologies. The modules were delivered using hypertext, digital content and three video production styles: slides with voice-over, talking heads and interviews. The main contribution of this work is the roadmap on how to design a highly relevant MOOC on privacy by design and the GDPR aimed at an heterogeneous audience.

1 Introduction

The General Data Protection Regulation (GDPR) is the EU regulation that aims to protect the *"fundamental rights and freedoms of natural persons and in particular their right to the protection of personal data"* and lays down *"rules relating to the protection of natural persons with regard to the processing of personal data and rules relating to the free movement of personal data."* [5] The regulation has a broad territorial scope and applies to the processing of personal data of people

This work was partially funded by WISR 16, Web-based Courses for International positioning of Strategic Research Groups, a project in the NU 16 Programme for Web-based International Education of the Knowledge Foundation (KKS) of Sweden.

L. Drevin and M. Theocharidou (Eds.): WISE 2018, IFIP AICT 531, pp. 95–107, 2018.
https://doi.org/10.1007/978-3-319-99734-6_8

who reside in the EU, regardless of whether the processing of their data takes place in the EU or not. It gives the supervisory authorities discretion to apply administrative fines of up to €20M or 4% of a company's total worldwide annual turnover (of its preceding fiscal reporting year, whichever is higher).

The GDPR was published in April 2016 and came into force on May 25th 2018. During the two-year transition period between its adoption and enforcement national governments had to transpose the GDPR into laws and organizations had to adapt to the regulation. The GDPR requires organizations to appoint a data protection officers (DPO) to oversee that the processing of personal data is compliant with the regulation, according to the cases specified under Art. 37–39 GDPR. DPOs are designated on basis of their professional qualities, including expert knowledge in data protection law and to provide advice and monitor the process of a data protection impact assessments (DPIA) required according to Art. 35 GDPR, an activity that requires legal, technical and organizational expertise. Besides, it will also be expected that a DPO can advise organizations in regard to their obligations to implement data protection by design pursuant to Art. 25 GDPR. As a consequence, the GDPR created a sudden demand for qualified professionals on technical, organizational and legal data protection aspects.

In order to serve this sudden educational demand, we designed a course on the GDPR and Privacy by Design (PbD) principles and legal and technical requirements. We set as objective to educate professionals and full-time undergraduate students using a single course structure. Therefore, we implement the course as a massive open online course (MOOC) that supports the individual learning behaviors and needs of an heterogeneous audience.

In this paper we describe how we designed this MOOC and present our lessons learned. We explain the overarching course structure and its organization into five modules, introduce the learning outcomes, and discuss the implemented teaching and learning activities.

This paper is organized as follows. Section 2 provides an introduction to the PbD course. Its modules, content and learning outcomes are outlined in Sect. 3. The teaching methods and the characteristics of the produced course content are described in Sect. 4. Section 5 presents the related work. The PbD course is discussed in Sect. 6 and Sect. 7 concludes the paper.

2   Designing the PbD Course

The course requirements were elicited by a core of data protection specialists from both academia and industry. This group was responsible to outline the learning outcomes of the course, structure it to address the needs of an heterogeneous audience constituted of professionals and undergraduate students, and reach out for a broad diverse and international audience.

Concerning the **intended audience and outreach**, the MOOC general model offers the desired tools for providing access to the course material to a large (and theoretically unbounded) audience. A MOOC also provides flexibility regarding the participants' individual learning pace, allowing them to decide

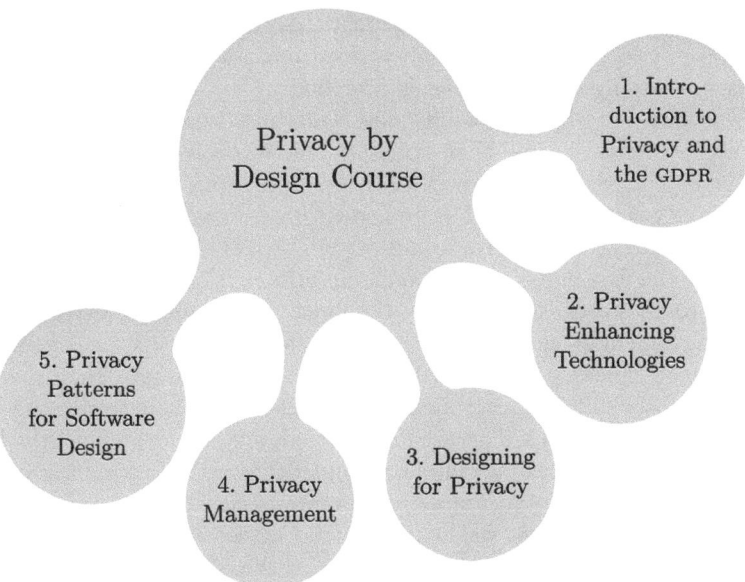

Fig. 1. The PbD course structure and its five modules.

upon their weekly effort devoted to the course, and adjust their attendance to their ongoing professional and academic commitments. The intended audience is undergraduate students and professionals with basic technical background in information technology (IT).

The **course content** covers topics on PbD, the GDPR and its application. The topics covered were chosen based on the course responsible experts' considerations about relevant legal, technical and organizational needs of a professional to demonstrate knowledge and competence on tasks assigned to a DPO.

The **course structure** is build on modules. The division into modules has a threefold objective: (*a*) the course content is divided into specific topics within the scope of PbD and the GDPR. It allows the course participants to select which modules to attend or to prioritize; (*b*) the required effort per module is bounded to 40 h. This requirement is key for course participants coming from industry, who can then better plan their work and study schedules, and in some cases claim the effort spent on the module as competence development; and (*c*) apply specific pedagogical tools and methods that better suits the course content and the learning outcomes defined for each module.

Figure 1 illustrates the five course modules. Participants who are interested in all modules, are recommended a sequential learning path: "1. Introduction to Privacy and the GDPR", "2. Privacy Enhancing Technologies" (PETs), "3. Designing for Privacy", "4. Privacy Management", and "5. Privacy Patterns for Software Design". Modules 1–2 cover the introductory topics (privacy fundamentals, GDPR and PETs) that the course is built upon. Modules 3–4 refer to PbD and the general knowledge on tools and methods required by the GDPR. Module 5 covers privacy in the context of software design. At the start of modules 3–5, a summary of the first two modules is provided.

The structure of the course into those modules was decided to make the course also attractive to full-time students and to professionals from industry and public sector, who may attend the course part-time and are able to select the modules that augment and complement their expertise. For instance, an experienced software developer would probably benefit most from the PbD course by attending the first three and the fifth modules.

The modules were assigned and developed by subgroups of this article's authors, which includes academic teachers and data protection specialists having technical, legal, industry and academic backgrounds, some of whom had been following the discussions around the GDPR and its development since the release of its first proposal in 2012. The modules were developed independently, having each a specific set of learning outcomes and delivered using a suitable set of pedagogic and presentation teaching techniques. Nonetheless, the overall course objective and course content was discussed and agreed upon in the team.

Most of the course content is **accessible** for those with (somewhat limited) physical or psychological impairment. All videos produced either are provided with scripts or have subtitles (or both). The platform used in the course lacks native text-to-speech capabilities but supports third-party solutions. They were not deployed in the initial deployment of the course.

The **course accreditation** is provided by the academic authors' home institution, which provides course examinations and grades in the form of European Credit Transfer and Accumulation (ECTS) credits for the participants enrolled in the course and on individual modules (1.5 ECTS/module).

The **assessment** of the participants is based on individual assignments and a short oral exam. Assignments are uploaded by the participants to the online course platform. Each module has its own assignment, and the expected effort to complete it is approximately eight hours. The oral exam has a twofold objective: assessment and checking for authorship. When uploading their assignments, the participants book their oral exams. Before the oral examination, the reports are checked for plagiarism and corrected. Oral exams are 10-min interviews using an online communication platform with video feedback.

The PbD course contents were distributed following a **Creative Commons Attribution license**, which allows all course content to be shared and adapted as long as appropriate credit is given and changes are indicated.

3   Modules, Content and Learning Outcomes

In this section, we describe the course modules, content and learning outcomes.

3.1   The Course Modules and Their Content

1. Introduction to Privacy and the GDPR covers the definition, history, and foundations of privacy, highlighting privacy challenges surrounding modern

Information and Communication Technology. The primary focus of the module is on the legal European framework on privacy, data protection, and cyber security. It includes agreements for transfer of personal data outside of the EU. Selected European Court of Justice decisions are discussed. The content is divided into the following five areas of knowledge:

1. The fundamentals of privacy, including the right to privacy, basic principles, laws and history, and key court decisions.
2. Contemporary privacy issues, including mobile computing, smart metering, social networks, big data, and cloud computing.
3. The GDPR, including its background, scope, definitions, basic principles, lawfulness and consent, data subject rights and responsibilities, and rules for data controllers and data processors.
4. The ePrivacy draft regulation and its possible implications.
5. The mapping from GDPR legal privacy principles to PETs.

2. Privacy Enhancing Technologies (PETs) introduces security and privacy mechanisms and technologies and details how security and privacy mechanisms can be used to solve practical and theoretical problems, along with discussions of their advantages and disadvantages.

1. An introduction to PETs, computer and network security basics and tools, and terminology for security and privacy.
2. Secure communication protocols and architectures, including PGP, TLS, Certificate Authorities (CAs), digital certificates and secure messaging.
3. Anonymous communication protocols (mainly Mix networks and Tor).
4. Databases and privacy, including k-anonymity and differential privacy.
5. Other relevant PETs and security technologies, such as blockchains, anonymous credentials, and Transparency Enhancing Technologies (TETs).

3. Designing for Privacy introduces the foundations of privacy, data protection, and privacy enhancing technologies, and then focuses on the concepts of privacy by design and privacy impact assessments (PIAs) by exploring the relevant background, their relationship to the foundation and fundamental human rights, and by introducing relevant methods.

1. Fundamental concepts that summarize the GDPR and PETs.
2. The meaning behind designing for "privacy". Privacy in relation to data protection, PbD, privacy paradigms, technology in hostile states, privacy protection goals, data protection by design and by default [4].
3. Privacy and DPIA, PIA as a process, frameworks and PIA in practice.

4. Privacy Management deals with privacy management as part of an organization's information security management. It introduces approaches to privacy management, provides insight into a management approach and explains how privacy threats can be anticipated and mitigated.

1. Privacy management into the context of data protection, stakeholders, PETs, and privacy management approaches, e.g. PDCA (Plan–Do–Check–Act).

2. The concept of "managed privacy", including privacy management as a data processing administration task.
3. PIA and privacy risk analysis as integral part of privacy management, including threats to privacy and sources of risk information.
4. The concept of privacy controls and properties, selection and risk mitigation.

5. Privacy Patterns for Software Design deals with privacy aspects during software design. It focuses on architectural tactics and patterns as reusable conceptual solutions to recurring privacy problems. It outlines how are these concepts used in agile development in order to engineer privacy into software.

1. An introduction to software architecture and design.
2. Privacy design strategies and as quality attribute of software systems.
3. Privacy design patterns and applying them in agile development.
4. Privacy anti and dark patterns.

3.2   The Learning Outcomes

The learning outcomes were specified following the principle of constructive alignment [2] which aims at aligning learning outcomes, learning activities and examination [9]. The SOLO (structure of observed learning outcome) taxonomy [3] was used to express the expectations concerning the participants' level of understanding after concluding a module. The learning outcomes range from uni-structural to extended abstract level of the SOLO taxonomy.

Every module has its own set of learning goals. The first two modules (on fundamentals of privacy, the GDPR, and PETs) provide the underlying building blocks for the learning material that follows.

The **Introduction to Privacy and the** GDPR module learning goals are:

- *Give an account* of basic legal privacy concepts, regulations and principles, and of major court decisions at national and European level.
- *Analyze* privacy challenges and the risks of ICT and applications.
- *Map* legal privacy principles to technical privacy concepts.

The **Privacy Enhancing Technologies** module learning goals are:

- *Give an account* of the basic security and privacy enhancing technologies.
- *Relate* security and privacy goals to mechanisms and technologies.
- *Explain* when and how to apply different privacy enhancing technologies.

The **Designing for Privacy** module learning goals are:

- *Give an account* of the concepts of privacy, data protection, privacy enhancing technologies, privacy by design, and privacy impact assessment.
- *Relate* privacy by design to privacy, data protection, privacy enhancing technologies, and fundamental human rights.
- *Explain* how privacy by design and privacy impact assessments are used.

Table 1. Amount of minutes of novel audio & video material per module.

Module	Intro. Privacy and the GDPR	PETs	Designing for Privacy	Privacy Mngmt.	Privacy patterns	TOTAL
Video	184	135	106	—	115	540
Audio	—	—	24	—	—	24

The first learning objective of Designing for Privacy ("[g]ive an account of the concepts of privacy...") refers to the modules 1–2 and content introduced in module 3 (PIAs). This learning goal is included in the goals of the modules 4–5. At the beginning of modules 4–5 on a summary of the modules 1–3 is provided, and a summary of the modules 1–2 is given at the start of module 3.

The **Privacy Management** module learning goals are:

– *Give an account* of approaches for managing information privacy.
– *Apply* methods for managing information privacy.
– *Analyze* risks to information privacy.
– *Compare and select* privacy controls and methods.

The **Privacy Patterns for Software Design** module learning goals are:

– *List* relevant privacy patterns.
– *Apply* appropriate architectural tactics for privacy and privacy patterns in a given systems context and for a given set of privacy requirements.
– *Explain* the key principles of architectural tactics for privacy patterns.
– *Analyze* the usage/occurrence of privacy patterns in a given system context.

4 Teaching Methods and Course Deployment

The teaching methods are adapted to the course contents and the MOOC model. The techniques used to deliver the modules are hypertext, digital content and three video production styles: slides with voice-over, talking heads and interviews. The videos' length is in the range between four and twenty five minutes.

All modules were delivered using video and slides especially designed for the PbD course, with the exception of the "Privacy Management" module. All videos have the option for subtitles (provided by the video hosting platform). All course slides are available in their source file format (MS PowerPoint) and in **pdf** format under the CC BY 4.0 (attribution) license. The amount of minutes of novel audio & video material present in each module is shown in Table 1. The videos length range of the n = 65 produced videos is [1:24, 24:35] minutes, with (AVG = 7:40, SD = 4:17) and n̄ = 6:30, IQR = 4:09 (Q1 = 4:51, Q3 = 9:00).

All lectures are complemented with mandatory and optional reading material and self-assessment online quizzes. The optional reading material provides the literature and resources for further self-studies for the course participants that are interested on a given topic. In addition, all lectures from the modules "Introduction to Privacy and the GDPR" and "Privacy Patterns for Software Design" include transcripts. A discussion forum is embedded in the MOOC platform.

Introduction to Privacy and the GDPR uses two video production styles: alternate talking head and slides with voice-over, and interviews. The module content covers legal and social privacy debates. Alternating a talking head with slides with voice-over video style was deemed an appropriate format to deliver this module's content because it allows the audience to follow the lecturer's face and expressions when voicing her viewpoints, which conveys relevant information. Twelve lectures were produced using this video production style.

The video interviews featured legal and technical experts from a German Data Protection Authority,[1] the DPO from the main authors' home institution, and a specialist from the industry. The overall topic of the interviews is on challenges and solutions for applying the legal requirements, especially the GDPR, in practice. This module featured six interviews. In addition, this module uses two existing anecdotal videos as support material.

Privacy Enhancing Technologies uses three video production styles: slides with voice-over, alternate talking head and slides with voice-over, and interviews. The module content covers technical aspects. Slides with voice-over offers a fitting alternative for technical subjects as animations help to illustrate how security and privacy protocols, tools and mechanisms work. Seventeen lectures were produced using this video production style.

Alternate talking heads and slides are used in the two videos on TETs. TETs is a subject with a strong human-computer interaction aspect connected to its technical aspects. Therefore, we judged that lecturer's face and expressions may improve the teaching quality for these two videos. This module feature an interview with an specialist in Tor from the University College London and four external videos: three presentations from specialists in selected subjects and one animation on Mix-Nets.

Designing for Privacy uses two video production styles: slides with voice-over and interviews. The module content covers technical aspects. Three interviews were recorded in audio format only. The lectures on Tor and PbD principles were delivered following the flipped classroom paradigm [8], as these topics requires a deeper analysis and criticism than the rest of module's content. These lectures reflect on the provided reading material and are supported by an external video (of Ann Cavoukian on the PbD principles).

Privacy Management uses a hypertext-based approach with elements of blended learning [7] and follows the flipped classroom paradigm. It discusses, illustrates and reviews the mandatory reading material. This module is supported by three external videos.

Privacy Patterns for Software Design uses three video production styles: slides with voice-over, alternate talking head and slides with voice-over, and interviews. Slides with voice-over were used to cover to main module contents. The other video styles were used as support material for short introductions

---

[1] The Unabhängiges Landeszentrum für Datenschutz (ULD), Schleswig-Holstein.

Table 2. The video production styles used in the PbD course modules. The TOTAL row corresponds to the unique entries to each category. External videos include presentation from external experts, anecdotes, and animations.

Module	Talking head and slides with voice-over	Slides with voice-over	Interviews	External videos
Intro. Privacy	12	—	8	2
PETS	2	17	1	4
Design. Privacy	1	13	8	1
Privacy Mngmt.	—	—	—	3
Privacy Patterns	1	9	1	1
TOTAL (unique)	14	35	16	8

on the GDPR and PETs. The main module contents are delivered following the flipped classroom paradigm.

A summary of the number of videos in each module, sorted according to the production style used, is presented in Table 2.

4.1 Course Deployment

The PbD course is deployed using Canvas, an open-source Learning Management System (LMS) and MOOC platform. It is locally deployed and managed.[2] A discussion forum and sharing of hand-in-assignments (the latter only to the "Privacy Management" module) are elements from the platform that are present in the courses. These tools aim at increasing student participation and interaction, and also help to reduce the drop-out rate, as shown by Anderson et al. [1].

The videos are hosted by YouTube (www.youtube.com), but not publicly indexed, i.e., they do not return as result of searches and can only be reached with a specific link to the video. The PbD course is available at https://kau.se/cs/pbd.

4.2 Enrollment and Participants

The course opened in two stages. In mid-January 2018 it was available for enrolled students and in March 2018 it opened for the general (non-enrolled) public. We initially set a limit for 100 enrolled students/module (to accommodate for the limitations on examining student essays). The exception is "Introduction to Privacy and the GDPR" which was planned to accommodate additional participants. The total number of students enrolled per module shown in Table 3.

---

[2] Released under the AGPLv3 license (https://github.com/instructure/canvas-lms).

4.3   Examination

The PbD course has quizzes for formative self-assessment [10] in all its modules. The quizzes are either multiple choice of true/false statements. As pointed out in Sect. 2, the assessment of the participants is based on individual assignments and a short oral exam. In this section, we discuss the content of the assignments.

Table 3. Number of students enrolled in each module.

Module	Intro. Privacy and the GDPR	PETs	Designing for Privacy	Privacy Mngmt.	Privacy patterns	TOTAL (unique)
Enrolled	115	100	99	96	99	146
Completed	15	10	8	7	9	22

In **Introduction to Privacy and the** GDPR the assignment is the design of valid consent forms including privacy policy statements. The task is twofold: (*i*) to evaluate the consent forms used for social login with Facebook according to the legal requirements of the GDPR, taking into consideration the Guidelines of the Art. 29 Data Protection Working Party on Consent.[3] The goal is to point out the legal requirements of the GDPR, such as for consent (Art. 7 GDPR) and data protection by default (Art. 25 GDPR), are not met. And (*ii*) to discuss how user interfaces could be designed to be GDPR compliant. This exercise has a high practical relevance, as most consent forms (as in January 2018) are not yet fully GDPR compliant. This exercise also relates to basic privacy principles (Art. 5 GDPR) connected to the design of policy and consent forms.

In PETs the assignment evaluates the extended abstract level of understanding of a participant into two out of four selected topics. Additional literature is provided in form of academic papers, online manuals and reports. The assignment was designed in two parts: (*i*) to discuss the benefits and limitations of a PET (Tor or Let's Encrypt) and (*ii*) to analyze the properties and privacy guarantees offered when aiming for anonymizing the contents of database or to analyze and assess the privacy properties of a crypto currency (Bitcoin).

In **Designing for Privacy** the assignment focus on the deeper learning objectives of the module, namely having to analyze or evaluate one out of five selected topics discussed in the module, such as comparing and motivating preferences for one PIA framework over another, or arguing for why a particular type of security technology in a setting is a reasonable measure that should be taken for the data protection by design requirement in the GDPR being fulfilled.

The **Privacy Management** assignment is twofold: (*i*) a written essay on the handling of legacy data under the light of the GDPR and report on data

---

[3] Article 29 Data Protection Working Party: Guidelines on Consent under Regulation 2016/679, http://ec.europa.eu/newsroom/just/document.cfm?doc_id=48849.

protection and user consent aspects, and (*ii*) using a mobile dating application as a case study, and perform a partial privacy risk assessment.

In **Privacy Patterns for Software Design** the assignment covers applying privacy design strategies and privacy patterns. The course participants are asked to describe a system and the personal data processed in it. They are asked to elaborate on several privacy design strategies that could be applied in this context and explain potentially applicable patterns implementing them.

The first round of examinations for the enrolled students ended in June 2018. The total number that completed the course modules is shown in Table 3. Three participants completed all five modules and four only one module.

5   Related Work

To the best of our knowledge, one of the first academic courses for data protection professionals that implemented an interdisciplinary perspective was introduced at the Hochschule Ulm in 1988. The program evolved into a certification course program for professionals in data protection [6]. Its curriculum has three parts: legal, information security and privacy management. It is a three weeks full-time regular course. The technical aspects of this course, however, do not include PETs (only general IT security).

There are private offerings for GDPR courses.[4,5,6] They are shorter than our PbD and GDPR course and/or focus only on the GDPR principles and core obligations of DPOs (such as privacy management), while not sufficiently addressing technical aspects that are important for the PbD process, such as PETs.

The International Association of Privacy Professionals (IAPP) lists institutes that offer privacy-related courses.[7] In its list, the majority are offered by law schools. To the best of our knowledge, there is no other MOOC on PbD and the GDPR targeting both undergraduate students and professionals.

6   Discussion

The course was released in January 2018 to participants enrolled to it through the official channels and opened to the general public in March 2018. The difference between the two groups is that the enrolled students have their written assignments graded and receive ECTS credits upon the successful completion of the course. At the time of writing, not enough student feedback is available for meaningful quantitative conclusions to be reached. Nonetheless, in this section we discuss some insights from the feedback obtained so far and from the background of the students enrolled in the PbD course.

Target group: an objective of the course is to teach skills that are needed by DPOs to undergraduate students and professionals, including those with

---

[4] IT Governance. https://www.itgovernance.co.uk/.

[5] GDPR Firebrand Training. http://www.firebrandtraining.co.uk/courses/.

[6] Olive Group. https://gdprcourse.com/.

[7] https://iapp.org/resources/article/colleges-with-privacy-curricula/.

major legal background and IT professionals who aim for GDPR compliance. The PbD course curriculum blends the legal, technical and managerial skills. It was designed for an audience with basic IT knowledge, with an equivalent of a semester of upper education studies in computer science or other technical subjects related to IT, or equivalent work experience. The first cohort of enrolled students is mainly composed of IT professionals, DPOs, and undergraduates.

On-line teaching styles: the modularized structure of the course allowed for experimentation with multiple presentation styles within the course, as seen in Sect. 4. The content of the modules is delivered using various audio&video styles, and even a hypertext only module. The flipped classroom paradigm is present in three out of five modules. In our course evaluation, we plan to assess the impact of our pedagogic choices using the students' feedback as input data.

The interaction with students was, so far, low compared to teaching in classroom. This was expected in a self-paced, with student interaction happening only via the platform's forum or by email, which is the general case for MOOCs.

Limited student feedback was obtained from: (*a*) online feedback forms distributed by the university and (*b*) informally after examination and grading. All feedback was provided voluntarily. So far, it is positive, with participants pointing out their personal and professional needs for such course. All but one course participants favor video lectures over text only material, and short videos (up to 10 min) were preferred rather than to long videos. The results from the online feedback forms are available at: https://www3.kau.se/kurstorget/. Feedback is nonetheless limited, with a small subset of participants completing the (anonymous) feedback forms. Praise on the course material was received from the industry, public sector agencies, and colleagues from universities in Sweden, Germany, Italy and Switzerland.

7   Conclusions

With the PbD course, we produced and deployed the first open, free, online course on interdisciplinary aspects of privacy, PbD and the GDPR. The course includes legal, technological and IT management perspectives. It is designed to capacitate IT professionals and undergraduate IT students with knowledge required by DPOs. It enables self-paced studies both in and out an academic program.

By opening the course to the general public we not only reach a much broader audience but also opened another channel to collect feedback to our teaching material and methods. By providing the PbD course in the GDPR transition year, we expect to provide an invaluable support not only to all course participants but to the whole society.

References

1. Anderson, A., Huttenlocher, D., Kleinberg, J., Leskovec, J.: Engaging with massive online courses. In: Proceedings of the 23rd International Conference on World Wide Web. ACM (2014)
2. Biggs, J., Tang, C.: Teaching for Quality Learning at University. McGraw-Hill Education, New York (2011)
3. Biggs, J.B., Collis, K.F.: Evaluating the Quality of Learning: The SOLO Taxonomy (Structure of the Observed Learning Outcome). Academic Press, New York (1982)
4. Danezis, G., et al.: Privacy and data protection by design. Technical report, Enisa (2014)
5. European Commission: Regulation (EU) 2016/679 of the European Parliament and of the Council of 27 April 2016 on the protection of natural persons with regard to the processing of personal data and on the free movement of such data, and repealing Directive 95/46/EC (General Data Protection Regulation). Official Journal of the European Union (2016)
6. Kongehl, G.: Das Ulmer Modell. Datenschutz und Datensicherheit **31**(5), 330–332 (2007)
7. MacDonald, J.: Blended Learning and Online Tutoring: Planning Learner Support and Activity Design. Gower Publishing, Ltd., Aldershot (2008)
8. Mazur, E.: Peer Instruction: A User's Manual. Series in Educational Innovation. Prentice Hall, Upper Saddle River (1997)
9. Moon, J.: Linking levels, learning outcomes and assessment criteria. In: Ministerial Conference of the European Higher Education Area (EHEA), vol. 12 (2005)
10. Scriven, M.: The methodology of evaluation. In: Perspectives of Curriculum Evaluation. AERA Monograph Series on Curriculum Evaluation. Rand McNally (1967)

Forming the Abilities of Designing Information Security Maintenance Systems in the Implementation of Educational Programmes in Information Security

Vladimir Budzko, Natalia Miloslavskaya$^{(\boxtimes)}$, and Alexander Tolstoy

The National Research Nuclear University
MEPhI (Moscow Engineering Physics Institute),
31 Kashirskoye shosse, Moscow, Russia
{NGMiloslavskaya, AITolstoj}@mephi.ru

Abstract. The paper shares the NRNU MEPhI's experience in forming the abilities to design the Information Security Maintenance Systems (ISMaS) in training Bachelors, Masters and Engineers in the field of Information Security (IS). It is proposed to form their abilities and teamwork skills when executing a course project by a team of students under supervision of their Professor within the framework of the "IS Management" discipline. Course projects help to reinforce the students' theoretical knowledge and develop their ability to apply this knowledge to the solution of practical problems. They are assigned at a group basis and in our case are aimed at designing the ISMaS of a particular object, which automates the implementation of a separate organization's process. A brief description of the process model for ensuring IS of such objects is given and the regulations for implementing the course project are presented in detail, indicating the types of abilities that are gained at each stage.

Keywords: Information security · Professional competencies · Abilities
System · Processes · Educational programme

1 Introduction

The implementation of educational programmes in the field of information security (IS) is aimed at the formation of specific professional competencies. This approach is consistent with the set of requirements that employers place on professionals in any field of professional activity, including IS [1–4]. A competency is traditionally referred to a combination of observable and measurable knowledge, skills and abilities, as well as individual attributes and work experience that contribute to enhanced employee performance and ultimately result in organizational success [5]. Knowledge is the cognizance of facts, truths and principles gained from formal training and/or experience. A skill is a developed proficiency or dexterity in mental operations or physical processes that is often acquired through specialized training; using the skills results in successful performance. An ability is the power or aptitude to perform physical or mental activities that are often affiliated with a particular profession. The ability to apply knowledge and

L. Drevin and M. Theocharidou (Eds.): WISE 2018, IFIP AICT 531, pp. 108–120, 2018.
https://doi.org/10.1007/978-3-319-99734-6_9

skills in a productive manner, which can be characterized by such behavioral attributes as aptitude, initiative, willingness, communication skills, team participation, leadership and others, shows the professional's effectiveness.

The goal of this paper is to describe our experience in forming the students' abilities and teamwork skills based on the implementation of a comprehensive course project for developing the IS Maintenance System (ISMaS) for a specific object to be protected. To achieve this goal, the process model of ensuring IS is considered, the regulations for the course project implementation are described and the results of implementing these regulations are analyzed on the example of training Bachelors, Masters and Specialists in the field of IS at the NRNU MEPhI (Russia).

2 Related Work

The efforts to develop a common approach to the formulation of requirements for IS competencies are being made worldwide for a long time. For example, an attempt to define a set of information and its structure, which created a basis for understanding terms and competencies in a particular knowledge area, was made in [6, 7]. The first steps to develop a common point of view refer to the World International conferences on IS Education (WISE) in the late 1990 s – early 2000 s. As a continuation, we have already presented our analysis of the three current basic approaches (American, Australian and European) [5, 8]. At the same time, several models of competency requirements for different organizations (such as CISA, CISSP, GIAC, etc.) have been developed for the certification of IS professionals.

For all available information sources, a common feature is answering "What is the formulation of a specific attribute of a specific professional competence?" question. They do not answer "How to form a professional competence?" question. We see two reasons why. On the one hand, the formation of the level of such attributes as "knowledge" and "skills" is well tested in the framework of traditional training forms: lectures, classes (seminars and labs) and students' independent work [5]. For example, for the "knowledge" attribute, one can use the recommendations of the SANS Institute [9]. On the other hand, there are some difficulties in the formation of the "skills" attribute in the framework of the typical educational process. The latter factor confirms the relevance of the results presented here. They should be considered as a continuation of our research on IS professional competencies presented in [5].

As for the other universities, which teach the full-time (not online) "IS Management" discipline, one can name the Norwegian University of Science and Technology (Norway), the City University of London (UK), the University of Pretoria (South Africa), the Eastern Kentucky University (USA), etc. But their Professors' publications do not describe any detail of the formation of abilities within this discipline.

3 Is Ensuring Process Model

In this paper, the term "*IS of an object*" refers to the state of the object's security against threats in the information sphere (formed on the basis of [10–13]). The *object* itself can be an information asset, IT or informatization object (object of applying IT to the main business processes of a particular organization such as an information system, automated system, automated process control system, etc.). To ensure this state is possible when performing specific actions, corresponding to a set of processes. This involves the following important terms. *Ensuring object's IS* (EIS) refers to the processes of maintaining the secure state of the EIS object. The *IS maintenance system* (ISMaS) is a set of corresponding EIS processes and IS controls, as well as the resources supporting them. In the Russian language the "maintenance" term is essentially broader than "management" as it means "ensuring" in all its possible senses, including corresponding system, staff, tools, documentation, procedures, etc.

Herein, the key terms are "a process" and "the process approach" [14]. A *process* is a set of interrelated and/or interacting activities, which are used to obtain the intended result. The *process approach* relates to a situation, where successive and predictable results are achieved more effectively and efficiently, and the activities are realized and managed as interrelated processes within a coordinated system. To structure all the processes, the cyclic Shewhart-Deming model or the Plan-Do-Check-Act (PDCA) cycle is traditionally used [15]. The PDCA cycle's application in various fields allows the effective management of activities on a systemic basis. This cycle can be applied within each organization's high-level process, as well as the separate production processes, and also the complete system of processes. It is closely connected with the planning, implementation, management and continuous improvement of both the organization's business processes and other processes related to its activities, including the EIS processes.

Each process as an integral part of the ISMaS must be appropriately managed. Any managerial action is also a process. It is aimed at ensuring the proper completeness and quality of the process, to which the managerial action is directed. Therefore, two groups of processes should be identified: the processes ensuring IS and the processes of their management. Their connectivity allows combining them into two systems: the IS System (ISS) (integrates the processes ensuring IS) and the IS Management System (ISMS) (integrates the management processes) [16, 17]. The *ISS* is a set of EIS processes, IS controls and resources needed to implement them. The *ISMS* is a set of management processes aimed at ensuring the completeness and quality of EIS processes (designed to plan, implement, monitor and improve the EIS processes), IS controls and resources supporting them. The ISMS should be considered as a part of the object's management system and it is aimed at planning, implementing, monitoring and improving the ISMaS. The PDCA cycle is applicable for both ISMaS management as a single process and for managing a separate ISS process.

The first group of ISMS processes forms four directions: planning, implementing, monitoring and improving the ISMaS as a single process. In this paper, only the "Planning" IS management processes are considered to determine the input and output data for separate components of the object's ISMaS as a single process. This direction unites all the processes which are necessary for the transition to the "Implementation" direction. In its essence, the "Planning" direction provides the ISMaS development.

In accordance with the recommendations of [10, 18–21], eight related subprocesses performing the ISMaS planning can be proposed (Fig. 1): "Object description", "Asset identification", "IS threat analysis", "Choice of IS threats", "IS threat description", "IS risk treatment", "IS Policy development", "Development of internal IS documents". In [13] we describe all of them in detail and so do not repeat this here. The connection between these subprocesses is due to the fact that the results of implementing any of them in the form of output data are the input data for the subsequent subprocess.

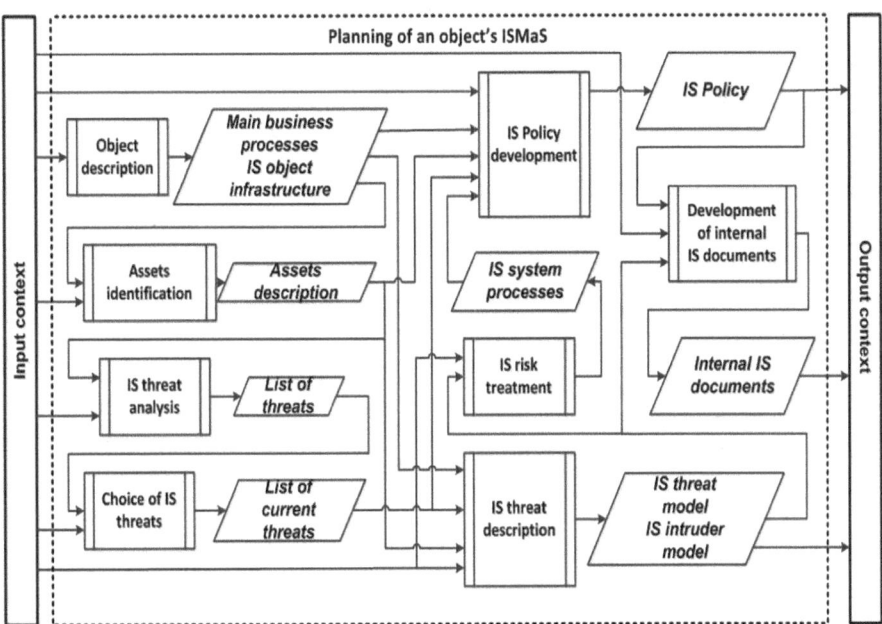

Fig. 1. Structural diagram for "Planning" of the ISMaS as a single process

The final result of designing the ISMaS for an individual object is its project documentation as a set of internal documents. An exemplary list of documents is the following [13]: "The list of the object's assets to be protected", "The list of the object's current IS threats", "The object's IS threats model", "The object's IS intruders model", "The object's IS risks registry", "The object's IS Policy", "The private IS policies related to the specific EIS processes at the object".

To obtain abilities in designing the ISMaS, a student must participate in designing all ISMaS subprocesses (Fig. 1).

4 Our Regulations for Forming the Abilities

Within the educational process for a specific curriculum, the ISMaS processes can be studied within the "IS Management" discipline. Traditional forms of discipline mastering (lectures, seminars) do not allow to fully form the abilities of each student to develop all the above-mentioned ISMaS subprocesses. In this case, an additional educational form such as an execution of a course project entitled "Designing the ISMaS for a specific object" is proposed. The number of subprocesses (8) requires a team of executors (students) to perform the course project successfully. Our regulations of the course project's implementation is shown in Fig. 2. Let us consider them in detail.

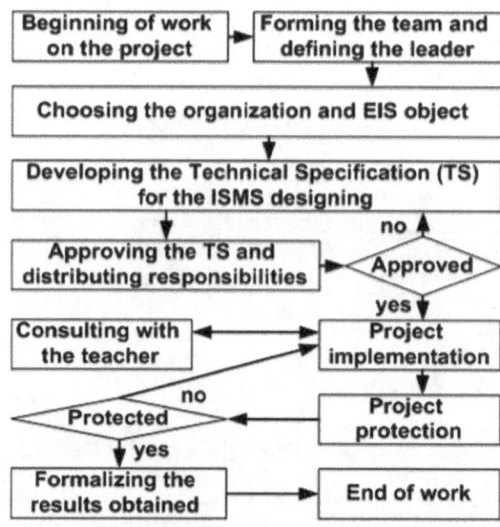

Fig. 2. The regulations for forming the abilities

1. *The beginning of work on the project* is determined by the completion of study the modern EIS approach, based on the process model. At the lectures students gain knowledge on the basics of IS management, and at the seminars they form their abilities and skills to apply the process approach to the ISMaS development. Thus each step of the regulations forms certain abilities corresponding to this particular step.
2. *The forming of the teams for individual course project's execution.* Students are distributed to separate teams voluntarily, taking into account the relations established in their groups. The number of students in one team is determined by the specifics of curriculum for training professionals (this issue is discussed in Sect. 5), qualification requirements for graduates, as well as the requirements of the discipline's syllabus. It is necessary to determine a team leader, whose duty is to coordinate work of all team members. The choice of the team leader is best entrusted to the team members. If there is a problem with this choice, it is made by their teacher.

3. *The choice of an organization and EIS object* is carried out by each team independently within the parameters set by their teacher with his/her consultative support. Students get the main recommendations for that at the seminars. For the given approach, students are recommended to choose as their EIS objects some organization's part, which deals with automated information processing under IS threats in the information sphere. For the selection of such EIS objects, students must know how to use IT for automated information processing.

4. *The development of the Technical Specification* (TS) for the ISMaS design. In the TS, the ISMaS requirements, structure and project documentation, which should be developed as a part of the course project, are defined taking into account the organization's peculiarities (its main business processes) and the EIS object (IT used). In this case, students should know the basic requirements for the TS writing and have the ability to use the relevant regulatory documents. In the collective implementation of this stage, students will gain the abilities in developing the TS document (the initial ISMaS design stage). At this stage, the precise duties and tasks for each team member are formulated.

5. *The TS approving and the distribution of responsibilities* are carried out at the seminar in the form of a talk with a slideshow by the leader of each team in the presence of students of the entire group, from which the separate teams are formed. During such seminars, the teacher organizes the active participation of all the students in discussing the results of the TS development by formulating questions to the acting team leader and making their comments. Based on the discussion of a specific TS and taking into account the comments made, the teacher decides whether to approve the TS or not. If the TS is not approved, the team should return to the TS development with its subsequent presentation. At this stage, students gain the abilities of public protection of their decisions, as well as the abilities to participate in discussions.

6. *The project implementation* consists of the steps, within which each team member performs his tasks in accordance with the TS approved at the previous stage and the structure of the associated ISMaS design subprocesses defined above (Fig. 1). The connections and recommended order of this process implementation are important.

The subprocess A "Object description" [13]. The results of its implementation are the descriptions of the organization's main business processes and the EIS object's infrastructure. Understanding the importance of the reliability and completeness of the description of the organization and the EIS object allows recommending all team members to take part in the implementation of this subprocess. At the same time, students gain the abilities in the analysis of specific EIS objects.

The subprocess B "Asset identification" [13] is intended for the description of the EIS objects, ensuring IS of which should be done by the ISS processes. Such objects are assets that are valuable to the organization and relate to the EIS object and to the main organization's business processes. Assets include information assets (open (public) information and restricted access information) and assets related to the processing environment (software and hardware components of the EIS objects). The subprocess's input data is the output of the previous subprocess A. The output of the subprocess can be issued as a separate document: (1) Linking the asset to a specific main business process implemented by the organization and to the EIS object's infrastructure; and (2) The asset description (its type, vulnerabilities and IS properties to be protected with their priorities if possible). During the subprocess implementation students gain the abilities to identify the objects (assets) to be protected and describe there IS-related characteristics.

The subprocess C "IS threat analysis" [13] is intended for the formation of a preliminary list of IS threats typical for the EIS object as a part of the organization. Each IS threat is associated with a separate asset and with the possibility of disrupting its IS properties that can cause damage to the organization. The subprocess's input data is the output of the subprocess B. Within the subprocess, the expert assessments based on the experience of ensuring IS for similar objects, as well as the expert assessments of applicability of typical IS threats listed in some normative documents or published in various sources are used. The expert assessment of this information allows determining a preliminary list of IS threats for the selected EIS object. The output data of the subprocess can be documented as "The preliminary list of IS threats to the assets of the EIS object". During the subprocess implementation students develop the abilities to assess IS threats specific to the selected EIS object, using various sources.

The subprocess D "Choice of IS threats" [13] generates a list of current IS threats specific to the EIS object of a particular organization. The subprocess's input data is the output of the subprocess C. For the selection of IS threats, the methodology for assessing the IS risks is used. Students get recommendations for using specific methods at the seminar, taking into account the provisions of ISO/IEC 27005 [21]. This method allows to determine the value of acceptable risk of violating the organization's main business processes (the so-called "risk appetite"), to assess the risks for each IS threat from the preliminary list of IS threats (subprocess C), and form a list of current IS threats, for which their risks exceed the risk-appetite. The result of the subprocess implementation is documented as "The list of current IS threats to the EIS object". Students develop the abilities to assess the risks of implementing IS threats for the selected EIS object.

The subprocess E "IS threat description" [13] is intended for the development of the IS threat and IS intruder models for the EIS object. The subprocess's input data is the output data of the subprocesses A, B and D. The description of IS threats to the assets of the EIS object can be performed in accordance with the recommendations [21], which for each IS threat from the list of current IS threats assume the definition of IS threat sources and method of its implementation, the asset (assets) to which this IS threat is directed, and the consequences of its implementation for these assets, as well as the damage to the main organization's processes. Within the subprocess, the quantitative value of risk for each IS threat must be calculated. This description should be done in "The IS threats model for the EIS object". If the IS threat's source is an intruder, the IS threat description should be supplemented with his description. At the same time, for each IS intruder its type (external/internal), the asset affected by him, the level of access to the assets and the way of influencing them, his motivation, qualifications and resources available should be determined. The description of IS intruders is presented in "The IS intruders model for the EIS object". It should be noted that the structures and contents of both models must be consistent and not contradictory to each other. When implementing the subprocess, students gain the abilities to develop the models of IS threats and intruders for the selected EIS object.

The subprocess F "IS risk treatment" [13] is designed to select IS controls, which implement separate EIS processes related to the ISS and reducing IS risks to an acceptable level. The subprocess's input data is the output of the subprocess E. Within the subprocess, for each current IS threat the EIS processes (the ISS is formed) and the IS controls, which form these processes, are selected with the assessment of residual IS risks. The process of their selection continues until the residual IS risk will be not higher than the risk appetite. The results of the subprocess implementation are formalized in "The IS risks registry", where the selected EIS processes, IS controls and the levels of initial and residual risks are shown for each IS threat. During the sub-process implementation, students gain the abilities to select the specific processes, IS controls for the real-world EIS objects, as well as the abilities to use some methodology for assessing the IS risks.

The subprocess G "IS Policy development" [13] is aimed at the development of the "The object's IS Policy" document (this is the output of the subprocess) as a normative document, which defines the requirements for EIS, the system of measures or the procedures for actions, as well as the responsibility of the organization's employees and control mechanisms for the defined area of EIS. The subprocess's input data is the output data of the subprocesses A, B, D, E and F. During the seminars, students develop the ability to define the structure and formulate the requirements for the IS Policy's content. When implementing the subprocess, the abilities to develop the "The object's IS Policy" are gained.

The subprocess H "Development of internal IS documents" [13]. The subprocess's input data is the output data of the subprocesses E, F and G. The nomenclature of the documents being developed is defined in "The object's IS Policy" and the TS for the ISMaS development. This set of documents should contain normative documents with the requirements for all EIS processes, as well as the implementation, operation, monitoring and improvement of the ISMaS. The results are presented as the private IS policies, regulations, instructions, etc.

7. *The project protection* is carried out at the seminar at least 4 weeks prior to the last class of the semester in the form of a talk by all team members performing the course project, with a slideshow in the presence of students of their group. During such seminars, the teacher organizes the active participation of all students in dis-cussing the results of the project by formulating questions and commenting. Based on the results of the discussion of a particular course project and taking into account the comments made, the teacher decides whether to approve or not the project's results. In the second case, the team must return to the course project's imple-mentation with subsequent re-protection, but exactly in the time limits of the semester, during which the course project is carried out. At this stage, students gain the abilities of public protection of their decisions, as well as the abilities to par-ticipate in their discussion.

8. *The formalization of the project results obtained* is the final stage. Every team prepares a Report consisting of separate Chapters, containing reports of each team member reflecting his/her contribution to the overall course project. In the "Introduction" section, the team leader characterizes and assesses the contribution of each team member to the course project's implementation. In each section, its executor should provide information on how the specific process has been implemented, which normative documents have been used, and how its connections with the other subprocesses have been taken into account. If the result of execution of a part of the course project is a draft of some internal IS document, then it must be written in accordance with the existing norms for such type of documents. In general, the Report should be written taking into account the requirements for design documentation. The Report is supplemented by a slideshow, used by students during their course project protection. Taking into account the results of the TS approving and the protection of the course project's results, as well as the quality of the Report and the activity of students in the course project's implementation, the teacher assesses the work of each student performing the individual course project.

After all the students expressed a unanimous opinion that this method of consolidating the theoretical knowledge obtained was very useful and interesting for them.

5 Our Experience in Forming the Abilities

The described approach in forming the abilities in ISMaS designing has been tested for 3 years at the NRNU MEPhI within the following curricula in IS: for Bachelor (annual recruitment of 1 student group (B1) of 20 students); Masters (4 groups of 20 students each) and Specialists (Engineers) (4 groups of 20 students each).

Bachelors' training is conducted according to the "Automated Systems Security" educational programme. Masters' training is conducted in four programmes: "Application of Cryptology Methods in ISMS" (M1); " IS Maintenance for Key Information Infrastructure Systems" (M2); "Business Continuity and IS Maintenance" (M3) and "Information and Analytical Support of Financial Monitoring" (M4). Training of Specialists is conducted in two specialities: "IS of Automated Systems" (ISAS) and "Information and Analytical Security Systems" (IASS).

The NRNU MEPhI carries out training within the framework of the approved educational standards, competence models of graduates, curricula and programs of educational disciplines. The educational standards and competence models of graduates formulate professional competencies related to the ISMS design. According to them, a graduate after graduation should have the following abilities [5]:

- *Bachelor:* To participate in the IS policy implementation; To conduct analysis of the source data for designing the EIS subsystems and tools; To formalize working technical documentation taking into account existing normative and methodical documents;

- *Master:* To assess risks, formulate an IS Policy for the objects to be protected; To develop the EIS systems, complexes, tools and technologies; To carry out the justification of composition, characteristics and functionality of the EIS systems and tools for the objects to be protected on the basis of the Russian and international standards; To organize IS management; To develop drafts of organizational and administrative documents, business plans in the field of professional activity, technical and operational documentation for the EIS systems and tools;
- *Specialist (ISAS):* To develop and analyze design solutions to ensure IS for automated systems (ASs); To develop an IS policy for AS; To participate in the design of the ISMS for AS; To develop proposals for improving the ISMS for AS; To develop drafts of documents regulating the EIS activities for AS; To participate in the formation of the organization's IS Policy and to monitor the effectiveness of its implementation; To manage IS for AS;
- *Specialist (IASS):* To identify the main IS threats, to build and investigate the intruders models for computer systems; To carry out the selection of technology, tools, computer facilities and EIS tools for the creation of special Information and Analytical Systems (IASs); To develop drafts of normative, methodological, organizational and administrative documents regulating the functioning of special IASs and their EIS tools.

Each of the above curricula contains the "IS Management " discipline. But its content differs in accordance with a different set of professional competencies. As a result, a different set of abilities must be formed when training Bachelors, Masters and Specialists. Thus, the course projects as the obligatory part of the different curricula relate to the implementation of a limited set of ISMS design subprocesses (or to the partial design of the ISMaS). From the analysis of their lists of professional competencies it follows that the formation of the abilities while training Bachelors, Masters (M1 and M4 programmes) and Specialists (IASS speciality) can be limited to the development of IS threats and intruders models for a particular EIS object. A full set of subprocesses should be included in the course projects for training Masters (M2 and M3) and Specialists (ISAS speciality). In this case, it was considered advisable to develop within the course projects only one private IS Policy for the M2 programme (for example, the IS Incident Management Policy), 2–3 private IS policies for the M3 programme (for example, the IS Incident Management Policies, Internal/External IS Audit or IS self-assessment Plan, Continuity Policy for the EIS object) and 3–5 internal IS documents for the ISAS speciality (for example, the Regulations on the implementation of specific IS controls).

Table 1 shows the relationship of the listed ISMaS design subprocesses with the course projects for the given curricula ("+" and "−" mean that the subprocess is included or not included in the course project respectively; "+", "++" and "+++" reflect the different number of internal IS documents for subprocess H).

Table 1. ISMaS design subprocesses in different NRNU MEPhI's curricula

Subprocess	Curriculum						
	Bachelor	Master				Specialist	
	B1	M1	M2	M3	M4	ISAS	IASS
A "Object description"	+	+	+	+	+	+	+
B "Asset identification"	+	+	+	+	+	+	+
C "IS threat analysis"	+	+	+	+	+	+	+
D "Choice of IS threats"	+	+	+	+	+	+	+
E "IS threat description"	+	+	+	+	+	+	+
F "IS risk treatment"	−	−	+	+	−	+	−
G "IS Policy development"	−	−	+	+	−	+	−
H "Development of internal IS documents"	−	−	+	++	−	+++	−
Number of team members	3	3	5	6–7	3	6–8	3

Our analysis of the content and scope of students work in the implementation of individual subprocesses allows recommending the following distribution of the subprocesses according to the executors (E) of the course projects (members of one team): E1: A and B; E2: C and D; E3: E; E4: F and G; E5: H: Development of one private IS Policy; E6: H: Development of several documents for the implementation of various IS controls. The number of internal IS documents, being developed by one executor, must be agreed with the teacher in advance. With this in mind, the recommended number of executors in the team implementing the course project will depend on the subprocesses, the implementation of which is included in it. The corresponding numbers are given in the last line of Table 1.

6 Conclusion

Studies aimed at applying modern methods of forming students' professional abilities in a certain field of activity are relevant not only for science, but also of great practical importance. Their usage makes it possible to increase the effectiveness of educational process and to provide graduates of educational institutions with all necessary conditions for the acquisition of modern professional competencies. In this paper, we shared our experience in the development and practical use of the regulations for forming the abilities to design the ISMaS for individual objects and teamwork skills (for example to break the task down into steps, plan a strategy, manage time, handle issues that only arise in groups such as delegate responsibilities, listen to alternative ideas, resolve conflicts and reach consensus, coordinate efforts, integrate the contributions of multiple team members, etc.) based on the implementation of the course projects. For that purpose, we created the different versions of regulations, allowing to take into account the peculiarities of curricula for training professionals in the field of IS of various levels (Bachelors, Masters and Specialists).

Our approbation of these versions revealed certain findings that must be taken into account when improving the educational process at the NRNU MEPhI. The most important of them is the significant increase in the study time attributed to the students' independent work, which is needed for the course project's implementation. Secondly, the teacher's role in individual consulting of students is expanded. Thirdly, it is necessary to create conditions for teamwork of students to perform their course projects and publicly protect the results obtained, taking into account the combination of features of teamwork and individual responsibility for their part of the whole work.

In this regard, there is a need to develop tools that improve the efficiency of ISMaS design processes for individual objects. For example, the creation of databases of typical assets' vulnerabilities of considered objects to be protected, IS threats, EIS processes and organizational and technical IS controls, the development of templates for documents related to the ISMaS design, as well as the use of visualization tools for the ISMaS design processes (such work has already been started by us in [13]).

Further development of this work is aimed at the improvement of our educational process, taking into account the identified factors, as well as the development of tools for designing the ISMaSs.

Acknowledgement. This work was supported by the MEPhI Academic Excellence Project (agreement with the Ministry of Education and Science of the Russian Federation of August 27, 2013, project no. 02.a03.21.0005).

References

1. EN 16234-1:2016 "e-Competence Framework (e-CF) – A common European Framework for ICT Professionals in all industry sectors – Part 1: Framework" and CEN/TR 16234-2:2016 "... Part 2: User Guide"
2. Newhouse, W., Keith, S., Scribner, B., Witte, G.: National Initiative for Cybersecurity Education (NICE) Cybersecurity Workforce Framework, August 2017. https://doi.org/10.6028/NIST.SP.800-181. Accessed 22 June 2018
3. Cybersecurity Curricula 2017: Curriculum Guidelines for Post-Secondary Degree Programs in Cybersecurity. Version 1.0. Report by ACM, IEEE, AIS, IFIP, 31 December 2017. http://cybered.acm.org/. Accessed 22 June 2018
4. Cybersecurity Skills Gap. ISACA. http://www.isaca.org/cyber/PublishingImages/Cybersecurity-Skills-Gap-1500.jpg. Accessed 22 June 2018
5. Miloslavskaya, N., Tolstoy, A.: Designing degree programmes for bachelors and masters in information security. In: Bishop, M., Futcher, L., Miloslavskaya, N., Theocharidou, M. (eds.) WISE 2017. IAICT, vol. 503, pp. 14–26. Springer, Cham (2017). https://doi.org/10.1007/978-3-319-58553-6_2
6. Bishop, M., Engle, S.: Software Assurance CBK and University Curricula: 10th Colloquium for Information Systems Security Education. University of California at Davis, USA (2006). http://nob.cs.ucdavis.edu/bishop/talks/2006-cisse-1/swacbk.pdf. Accessed 22 June 2018
7. Theoharidou, M., Gritzalis, D.: Common body of knowledge for information security. IEEE J. Secur. Priv. 5(2), 64–67 (2007)

8. Miloslavskaya, N., Tolstoy, A.: ISO/IEC competence requirements for information security professionals. In: Bishop, M., Futcher, L., Miloslavskaya, N., Theocharidou, M. (eds.) WISE 2017. IAICT, vol. 503, pp. 135–146. Springer, Cham (2017). https://doi.org/10.1007/978-3-319-58553-6_12

9. Yusof, A.: Ways to Become an Effective Information Security Professional - From a GIAC Wannabe Perspectives. SANS Institute InfoSec Reading Room. Version: 1 (2001). https://www.sans.org/reading-room/whitepapers/infosec/ways-effective-informa-tion-security-professional-giac-wannabe-perspectives-601. Accessed 22 June 2018

10. ISO/IEC 27000:2018 Information technology – Security techniques – Information security management systems – Overview and vocabulary

11. Kissel, R.: Glossary of Key Information Security Terms. NIST Interagency/Internal Report (NISTIR), 7298rev2, May 2013. https://ws680.nist.gov/publication/get_pdf.cfm?pub_id=913810. Accessed 22 June 2018

12. GOST R 50922-2006 Information security. Main terms and definitions. (In Russian)

13. Miloslavskaya, N.G., Tolstoy, A.I.: Visualization of information security management processes. Sci. Visual. J. 9(5), 117–136 (2017)

14. ISO 9000:2015 Quality management systems – Fundamentals and vocabulary

15. Deming, W.E.: Out of the Crisis. MIT, Cambridge (1986)

16. Bank of Russia Standard STO BR IBBS-1.0-2014 Information Security Maintenance for Organizations of the Banking System of the Russian Federation. General Conditions. (In Russian)

17. GOST R 57580.1-2017 Security of financial (banking) operations. Protection of information of financial organizations. Basic composition of organizational and technical measures. http://www.cbr.ru/eng/analytics/Gubzi_docs_en/st-10-14_en.pdf. Accessed 22 June 2018

18. ISO/IEC 27001:2013 Information technology – Security techniques – Information security management systems – Requirements

19. ISO/IEC 27002:2013 Information technology – Security techniques – Information security management systems – Code of practice for information security controls

20. ISO/IEC 27003:2017 Information technology – Security techniques – Information security management systems – Guidance

21. ISO/IEC 27005:2011 Information technology – Security techniques – Information security risk management

Identifying the Cybersecurity Body of Knowledge for a Postgraduate Module in Systems Engineering

Sune von Solms[1(✉)] [iD] and Lynn Futcher[2] [iD]

[1] Department of Electrical Engineering Science,
University of Johannesburg, Johannesburg, South Africa
svonsolms@uj.ac.za
[2] School of Information and Communication Technology,
Nelson Mandela University, Port Elizabeth, South Africa
Lynn.Futcher@mandela.ac.za

Abstract. In the light of Industry 4.0, there exists a drive in engineering to include cybersecurity in the design, development and maintenance of smart cyber-physical systems. The high interconnectivity of these systems make these systems more susceptible to cyberattacks. In South Africa, the engineering education space does not traditionally cater for cybersecurity training in undergraduate or post-graduate studies. The lack of cybersecurity education in engineering and the need for cybersecurity knowledge in the industry highlights a knowledge gap in the field of cybersecurity engineering. This paper describes the process followed to determine the body of knowledge which should be considered for a postgraduate module in cybersecurity in engineering in South Africa. Findings show that topics related to Software Security, Systems Security and Organizational Security are deemed most important for inclusion in the cybersecurity body of knowledge for a postgraduate module in Systems Engineering.

Keywords: Cybersecurity · Curriculum design · Systems Engineering
Education · Postgraduate Education

1 Introduction

Industry 4.0, referred to as Industrial Internet of Things (IIoT) or the fourth industrial revolution, describes the use of new digitized and connected industrial systems [1]. In the light of these new developments, the systems designed by engineers are fundamentally changing. The interconnected nature of systems developed for Industry 4.0, called Industry 4.0-ready systems, means that cyberattacks can have extensive effects on these engineering systems – more so than in the past. Therefore, engineers designing, developing, managing and operating these systems should treat security as a key concern, incorporating security across the entire lifecycle from the start [2, 3].

The cybersecurity workforce worldwide is one of the fastest growing fields globally, with gaps in the workforce estimated to reach 1.8 million by 2022 [4–7]. South Africa (SA) is also low in cybersecurity professionals, evident from the number of cybersecurity engineering positions advertised and vacant [8]. Many students graduating from

L. Drevin and M. Theocharidou (Eds.): WISE 2018, IFIP AICT 531, pp. 121–132, 2018.
https://doi.org/10.1007/978-3-319-99734-6_10

engineering degrees in SA lack the cybersecurity knowledge and skills needed within their specific engineering industry as they often receive only an overview of cybersecurity [4, 9, 10]. The lack of cybersecurity content in South African engineering education creates a gap in cybersecurity knowledge amongst engineers in industry.

This paper describes the process followed to determine the body of knowledge which can be considered in a postgraduate cybersecurity module for Systems Engineering in SA. The paper is structured as follows: Sects. 1 and 2 present the introduction and background to the paper, while Sect. 3 discusses the research methodology followed. Section 4 highlights the significance to engineering education for the cybersecurity knowledge areas prescribed by the Curriculum Guidelines for Post-Secondary Degree Programs in Cybersecurity (CSEC2017). Section 5 presents feedback from engineering professionals relating to body of knowledge, where Sect. 7 concludes the paper.

2 Curriculum Development for the Cybersecurity Skills Gap

Industry and professional institutes are driving strategies to update engineering frameworks to include security. The National Institute of Standards and Technology (NIST) published the National Initiative for Cybersecurity Education (NICE) Cybersecurity Workforce Framework, providing guidance on workforce development, training and education of cybersecurity professionals [11]. The International Council of Systems Engineering (INCOSE) chartered a working group to update formal systems engineering processes to include security "as a fundamental part of system engineering" [12]. Engineering organizations are starting to recognize that security integration in engineering systems cannot only be limited to the IT industry, but that it must be included in software development, risk management, human factors and all other areas within an organization [13, 14]. There exists a high demand in cybersecurity professionals in the engineering space in SA, indicative that little progress has been made in the education space. Throughout academic institutions globally, only a handful of undergraduate and postgraduate degrees in cybersecurity exist. In SA, there are no known comprehensive engineering cybersecurity courses offered by South African universities, based on their undergraduate and postgraduate syllabus descriptions [10]. The lack of cybersecurity content or modules in SA engineering education and the need for cybersecurity professionals point toward a gap in cybersecurity knowledge amongst engineers in industry.

The CSEC2017 guideline provides comprehensive curricular guidance for cybersecurity education efforts. It aims to support the development of future programs and associated educational efforts at the post-secondary level [4]. This framework provides clear guidance which can be utilized in the development of cybersecurity courses in engineering in SA. CSEC2017 states that it should be used in collaboration with competencies defined in the workplace. Therefore, the development of an engineering cybersecurity module requires input from the engineering industry to ensure that the competencies and knowledge included in the module accurately map to the industry needs.

3 Methodology

The aim of this paper is to identify the knowledge areas to be included in a module to provide engineers with cybersecurity knowledge relevant to the industry. To ensure that the knowledge gained by engineering students are deemed relevant in the engineering industry, input from engineering professionals is required. The methodology followed in this study for the identification of cybersecurity content for engineers is shown in the four steps below. The 32-item checklist of the consolidated criteria for reporting qualitative studies (COREQ) was used as a guideline to ensure complete and transparent reporting, comprehensiveness and credibility of this research [15].

1. To investigate the qualification standard and educational requirements for post-graduate studies set out by the Department of Higher Education (DHET) in SA.
2. To determine the broad structure for module development set out in the CSEC2017 guidelines.
3. To investigate the CSEC2017 cybersecurity knowledge areas and how the content relates to the engineering profession, viewed through the disciplinary lens.
4. To construct a module outline, based on the CSEC2017 cybersecurity knowledge areas, relevant to a cybersecurity module in engineering.

Following the process set out in the COREQ criteria, steps 1 and 2 listed above was conducted to clarify the theoretical framework underpinning this study. This framework, discussed in Sect. 4, organizes the 8 knowledge areas in the CSEC2017 into a structured format to be used as a guideline in the elite interviews (step 3) [15, 16]. Elite interviews were selected as it advances the research process by gathering rich detail about key professional's thoughts and attitudes toward the research topic [17–19]. In-depth and semi-structured elite interviews were conducted to explore the experiences of participants in the engineering industry and academia and how it relates to the CSEC2017 framework [19, 20]. The design of the elite interviews as well as the analysis and findings are discussed in Sect. 5. Step 4, discussed in Sect. 5, follows a general inductive approach to summarize the data collected from the interviews; to determine the links between the research objectives and the findings; and finally to construct a module outline deduced from the collected data [20].

4 Towards Determining the Structure/Context for a Cybersecurity Engineering Module

4.1 Overview of South African Postgraduate Engineering Degrees

The Bachelor of Engineering (B.Eng) degrees in SA are structured to provide a coherent core in mathematics, natural sciences and engineering fundamentals for a solid platform for further studies [21]. The Higher Education Qualifications Sub-Framework (HEQSF) states that a B.Eng degree must provide graduates with a well-rounded, broad education to prepare them for "professional training, post-graduate studies or professional practice in a wide range of careers" [22]. The B.Eng program is structured so that engineers will be able to further deepen their knowledge on a specific, sub-discipline, or specialist topic as the need arises. As the B.Eng degree is structured toward a more general engineering knowledge base, the creation of degrees or modules dedicated to cybersecurity should be developed at the postgraduate level.

HEQSF stipulates two variants of a Master's degree: a research Master's degree by dissertation, or a Master's degree by coursework and mini-dissertation. A research Master's degree requires a student to complete a single advanced research project in a specialized field of study. A coursework Master's degree requires students to complete a coursework programme to provide a broad exposure to a field. Generally, engineering professionals from industry are more inclined to pursue a coursework Master's as it provides a broad understanding of the field of study. The University of Johannesburg (UJ) in SA is in the process of finalizing a coursework Master's degree in Systems Engineering with the aim to provide engineering professionals specialized systems engineering knowledge. As there exists a drive from industry to include security into the development of new engineering systems in general, the inclusion of a cybersecurity module for the Systems Engineering coursework Master's qualification is motivated.

4.2   Cybersecurity Curricular Guidelines

CSEC2017 indicates that cybersecurity programs require curricular content which includes the theoretical and conceptual knowledge essential to understanding the discipline. It states that the content which must be included in any cybersecurity program must have a balance of "breadth and depth, along with an alignment to workforce needs". The CSEC2017 model divides the cybersecurity content into 8 knowledge areas along with 6 cross cutting concepts. These knowledge areas and concepts must be viewed through a disciplinary lens which represents the underlying discipline which will form the foundation of the cybersecurity module, in this case, engineering [4].

Knowledge Areas. The 8 knowledge areas stipulated in the CSEC2017 include: Data, Software, Component, Connection, System, Human, Organizational and Societal Security. Each area contains a range of knowledge units and related topics. Apart from the 8 knowledge units and related topics included in a knowledge area, each knowledge area contains a number of essential topics which should be included in every cybersecurity program. These topics capture the skills and knowledge that all students introduced to cybersecurity should acquire, regardless of discipline or program focus and is CSEC2017 states that essential topics should be included early in cybersecurity programs and reinforced throughout. As the envisaged postgraduate cybersecurity module aims to introduce engineers to the concepts of cybersecurity, these essentials must be covered in the module. These topics are provided in Table 1.

Cross Cutting Concepts. CSEC2017 indicates that the knowledge areas are not mutually exclusive. There exist cross cutting concepts which provide students with an understanding of how the various knowledge areas relate to each other and reinforces the security mindset which they should possess. The 6 cross cutting concepts are: Confidentiality, Integrity, Availability, Risk, Adversarial Thinking and Systems Thinking. These concepts must be included throughout the envisaged engineering module.

Table 1. Overview of essential topics included in each Knowledge Area

Knowledge area	Essentials
Data Security	Basic cryptography concepts; Digital forensics; End-to-end secure communications; Data integrity & Authentication; Information storage security
Software Security	Fundamental design; Security requirements & role in design; Implementation issues; Static & dynamic testing; Configuring & Patching; Ethics
Component Security	Vulnerabilities of system components; Component lifecycle; Secure component design principles; Supply chain management security; Security testing; Reverse engineering
Connection Security	Systems, architecture, models, & standards; Physical component interfaces; Software component interfaces; Connection attacks; Transmission attacks
System Security	Holistic approach; Security policy; Authentication & Access control; Monitoring; Recovery and Testing; Documentation
Human Security	Identity management; Social engineering; Awareness & Understanding; Social behavioral privacy and security; Personal data privacy and security
Organizational Security	Risk management; Governance & Policy; Laws, ethics & compliance; Strategy & planning
Societal Security	Cybercrime and Cyber law; Cyber ethics; Cyber policy; Privacy

Disciplinary Lens. CSEC2017 states that a cybersecurity program must be created through the view of a specific disciplinary lens, representing the computing discipline relevant to the field of study. The planned module is for engineering professionals from the broad engineering discipline aiming to gain a Master's degree in Systems Engineering. Although the field of systems engineering cannot directly be associated with a computing discipline, the majority of systems developed today are highly-connected cyber-physical systems. Therefore, the disciplinary lens would be systems engineering.

5 Cybersecurity Knowledge Through the Engineering Lens

To determine the cybersecurity body of knowledge through the systems engineering lens, the CSEC knowledge units were presented to engineering professionals. Four in-depth and semi-structured elite interviews were scheduled, two with engineering professionals in academia (referred to as Academic 1 and Academic 2 in Tables 2, 3, 4, 5, 6, 7, 8 and 9) and two with engineering professionals in industry (referred to as Industry 1 and Industry 2 in Tables 2, 3, 4, 5, 6, 7, 8 and 9). All four participants are professionally registered engineers with ECSA, selected based on their knowledge of and experience in systems engineering. The participants were provided with information regarding the researchers and their affiliations, the nature of the research, how long the interview will take, how the data will be used and where the results will be anonymously disseminated [23]. A detailed table of all knowledge units in the 8 knowledge areas, summarized in Table 1, were constructed to use as a guideline for the elite interviews. Each participant were asked open-ended questions, followed-up by closed-ended questions, where the combination of open- and closed-ended questions enabled the participants provide their views in their own words, but also provided the structured data required to populate Tables 2, 3, 4, 5, 6, 7, 8 and 9 [23]. The participants were guided through the table and prompted to comment on the relevance of each knowledge unit to systems engineering as well as the depth of which they felt it should be included in the module. The results of these discussions are captured in Tables 2, 3, 4, 5, 6, 7, 8 and 9 below where the feedback is coded as follows:

- Essential (E): Included in depth in the module. All essential topics were automatically marked "E" for essential.
- Overview (O): Included to provide a high level knowledge on the topic.
- Too Technical (TT): Not included due to the high technical nature of the topic.
- Additional Content (AC): Relevant and nice to have as additional content.
- Not Relevant (NR): Topic not directly relevant to systems engineering as task might sit with another professional.

In addition to documenting the relevance of each knowledge unit, the researcher made notes detailing contextual details and quotes for data analysis and interpretation.

Data Security. This knowledge area includes topics related to the protection of data at rest, during processing, and in transit. A systems engineer should have a good understanding of the system as a whole, not necessarily details relating to technical aspects. A good overview is required to understand where and how this fits into the system.

Table 2. Data Security knowledge units' relevance to systems engineering discipline

Knowledge units	Academic 1	Academic 2	Industry 1	Industry 2
Essentials	E	E	E	E
Cryptography	TT	TT	O	O
Digital Forensics	O	O	O	O
Data Integrity and Authentication	E	E	E	O
Access Control	O	E	E	O
Secure Communication Protocols	TT	TT	E	O
Cryptanalysis	TT	O	E	O
Data Privacy	O	O	E	O
Information Storage Security	TT	TT	E	O

Software Security. This knowledge area covers the development and use of software to preserve the security properties of the information and systems it protects. This knowledge area is relevant to engineers developing Industry 4.0-ready systems as all these systems contain software to a certain extent.

Table 3. Software Security knowledge units' relevance to systems engineering discipline

Knowledge units	Academic 1	Academic 2	Industry 1	Industry 2
Essentials	*E*	*E*	*E*	*E*
Fundamental Principles	O	O	E	O
Design	E	E	E	E
Implementation	TT	O	NR	O
Analysis and Testing	O	O	NR	E
Deployment and Maintenance	O	O	NR	O
Documentation	AC	O	NR	O
Ethics	E	E	E	O

Component Security. This knowledge area covers topics relating to the design, procurement, testing, analysis and maintenance of components to be integrated into larger systems. A systems engineer should have a good understanding of the system as a whole, not necessarily the technical details relating to the components aspects.

Table 4. Component Security knowledge units' relevance to systems engineering discipline

Knowledge units	Academic 1	Academic 2	Industry 1	Industry 2
Essentials	*E*	*E*	*E*	*E*
Component Design	O	TT	NR	O
Component Fabrication	TT	TT	NR	TT
Component Procurement	TT	TT	NR	TT
Component Testing	TT	TT	NR	O
Component Reverse Engineering	TT	TT	NR	TT

Connection Security. This knowledge areas covers the aspects relating to securing the connections between components, including physical and logical connections.

A systems engineer does not necessarily have to have all the technical knowledge relating to connections, but rather a holistic view of the system.

Table 5. Connection Security knowledge units' relevance to systems engineering discipline

Knowledge units	Academic 1	Academic 2	Industry 1	Industry 2
Essentials	*E*	*E*	*E*	*E*
Physical Media	TT	TT	TT	O
Physical Interfaces and Connectors	TT	TT	TT	O
Hardware Architecture	O	TT	TT	O
Distributed Systems Architecture	E	TT	TT	O
Network Architecture	O	TT	TT	O
Network Implementations	TT	TT	TT	O
Network Services	TT	TT	TT	O
Network Defense	TT	TT	TT	O

Systems Security. This knowledge area contains topics relating to the security aspects of systems that are composed of components and connections, and use software. This knowledge area covers security from a system view, which is typically where the systems engineer operates from.

Table 6. Systems Security knowledge units' relevance to systems engineering discipline

Knowledge units	Academic1	Academic 2	Industry 1	Industry 2
Essentials	*E*	*E*	*E*	*E*
System Thinking	E	E	E	E
System Management	E	E	E	E
System Access	O	O	E	O
System Control	O	O	E	O
System Retirement	E	O	O	O
System Testing	E	E	O	E
Example System Architectures	TT	O	NR	O

Human Security. This knowledge area covers the protection of individuals' data and privacy in the context of organizations and personal life. As individuals will be responsible for the operation and use of the designed system, the human aspects cannot be ignored by a systems engineer.

Table 7. Human Security knowledge units' relevance to systems engineering discipline

Knowledge units	Academic 1	Academic 2	Industry 1	Industry 2
Essentials	*E*	*E*	*E*	*E*
Identity Management	O	O	E	O
Social Engineering	AC	O	NR	O
Personal Compliance with Cybersecurity Rules/Policy/Ethical Norms	AC	O	NR	O
Awareness and Understanding	AC	NR	E	O
Social and Behavioral Privacy	NR	NR	NR	O
Personal Data Privacy and Security	NR	NR	E	O
Usable Security and Privacy	NR	NR	E	O

Organizational Security. This knowledge area relates to the protection of organizations from cybersecurity threats and managing risk. As any systems engineer operates within an organization or develops systems to be used in an organization, aspects of the organizational security cannot be ignored.

Table 8. Organizational Security knowledge units' relevance to systems engineering discipline

Knowledge units	Academic 1	Academic 2	Industry 1	Industry 2
Essentials	*E*	*E*	*E*	*E*
Risk Management	E	E	E	E
Security Governance & Policy	E	E	E	O
Analytical Tools	O	TT	E	O
Systems Administration	NR	NR	E	O
Cybersecurity Planning	O	O	E	O
Business Continuity, Disaster Recovery, and Incident Management	O	NR	O	O
Security Program Management	E	O	O	O
Personnel Security	AC	O	E	O
Security Operations	AC	O	E	O

Societal Security. This knowledge area covers topics that has a broad impact on society as a whole. Any engineer must always be aware of the impact and ethics surrounding the developed systems.

Table 9. Societal Security knowledge units' relevance to systems engineering discipline

Knowledge units	Academic 1	Academic 2	Industry 1	Industry 2
Essentials	*E*	*E*	*E*	*E*
Cybercrime	O	O	O	O
Cyber Law	O	O	E	O
Cyber Ethics	E	E	O	O
Cyber Policy	AC	NR	E	O
Privacy	AC	NR	E	O

The first engineering professional from Industry (Industry 1), stated that one of the most important aspects of cybersecurity in systems engineering lies in the securing of data. Data includes personal data and information related to the working environment. Therefore, knowledge units in the Data Security, Systems Security and Organizational Security knowledge areas were marked as Essential. The second professional from Industry (Industry 2) stated that the System Thinking and Systems Requirements (within the Systems Security knowledge area) are essential for a systems engineer to know. The professional emphasized that a systems engineer should have a fair overview of all the cybersecurity knowledge areas in order to ask the correct questions, although the technical details are not required. A holistic view is more important than the technical detail. The first engineering professional from academia (Academic 1) stated that a holistic view is essential and underlined Systems Security and Organizational Security as the most important for inclusion in depth in the module. The professional agreed that, in order to obtain a solid holistic view of security, the essential topics for each knowledge area must be included. The second academic (Academic 2) underlined the importance of the Systems Engineering, especially System Thinking. The academic also stated that the highly technical knowledge units are not required.

6 Basic Outline of Cybersecurity Knowledge Areas for Postgraduate Engineering Studies

From the discussion in Sect. 5, a systems engineer needs to maintain a holistic view of the system. The technical details of data, component and communication security are not required in depth, but only a sufficient overview knowledge to understand the role each of these aspects play in the system. It can be argued that the systems engineer should be able to gain only an overview on Data Security, Component Security and Connection Security through the inclusion of only the essential topics. All interviewed professionals stated that a good overview of Human Security, Organizational Security and Societal Security are required in the module. Therefore, these three knowledge areas can be included in the module as overview knowledge units. The only exception is the knowledge unit of Cyber Ethics (within Societal Security), which all professionals feel must be covered in detail in the module as well as Risk Management and Security Governance & Policy (within Organizational Security).

In general, the knowledge areas of Software Security, Systems Security and Organizational Security were deemed the most important for in depth inclusion in the module. The majority of Industry 4.0-ready systems contain some form of software which the systems engineer must understand. System security was underlined as important in most interviews, except for the knowledge unit of Example System Architectures. The inclusion and exclusion of knowledge units are summarized in Table 10 below.

Table 10. Summary of knowledge units included and excluded in body of knowledge

Knowledge area	Knowledge units included	
	In depth	Overview
Data Security	Essential topics only	–
Software Security	Essentials; Fundamental Principles; Design; Ethics	Implementation; Analysis & Testing; Deployment & Maintenance; Documentation;
Component Security	Essential topics only	–
Connection Security	Essential topics only	–
System Security	System Thinking; System Management; System Testing	System Access; System Control; System Retirement
Human Security	Essential topics	All knowledge units
Organizational Security	Essentials; Risk Management; Security Governance & Policy	Remaining knowledge units
Societal Security	Essentials; Cyber Ethics	Remaining knowledge units

Table 10 provides the body of knowledge for a postgraduate cybersecurity module in Systems Engineering. The module includes the essential topics as prescribed in CSEC2017 as well as topics described by engineering professionals as essential.

7 Conclusion

The creation of systems to comply with Industry 4.0 environments requires highly connected systems which must be able to withstand various types of cyberattacks. There is a drive from the engineering industry to include cybersecurity into the engineering of systems to improve its inherent security. However, many systems engineers are not educated in the field of cybersecurity. Engineering students may receive a high level overview of cybersecurity concepts in some engineering modules, but courses seldom include specialization cybersecurity topics. This lack of cybersecurity content in SA engineering education creates a gap in cybersecurity knowledge amongst engineers.

This paper included an investigation to determine the body of knowledge for the creation of a postgraduate cybersecurity module in systems engineers. The CSEC2017 framework were utilized as a baseline for the module outline, and presented to engineering professionals to determine relevant body of knowledge for systems engineering. The knowledge areas were discussed with engineering professionals from academia and industry through interviews to determine which areas are considered essential for inclusion in the module. The basic body of knowledge for a postgraduate cybersecurity module is presented, which states that the knowledge areas of Software Security, Systems Security and Organizational Security were deemed the most important for in depth inclusion in the module along with the essential topics stipulated in the CSEC2017 document. The main limitation of this work is that this basic body of knowledge was guided by the input from only four professional participants, two from academia and two from industry. However, this is deemed sufficient for a preliminary investigation providing a baseline from which to work. Future work will include the collection of input from a broader spectrum of top-level professionals to inform the new postgraduate module in Systems Engineering.

References

1. Kiel, A.: What do we know about "Industry 4.0" so far? In: Proceedings of the International Association for Management of Technology (IAMOT 2017) (2017)
2. Morgan, S.: IBM's CEO On Hackers: "Cyber Crime Is The Greatest Threat To Every Company In The World" (2005). https://www.forbes.com/sites/stevemorgan/2015/11/24/ibms-ceo-on-hackers-cyber-crime-is-the-greatest-threat-to-every-company-in-the-world/#1baf053373f0. Accessed 9 Jan 2017
3. Tamura, E.: Hewlett Packard Enterprise Leads Transformation of Cyber Defense with "Build it In" and "Stop it Now" (2006). http://www8.hp.com/us/en/hp-news/press-release.html?id=2184147#.WtIU5S6uyUl. Accessed 9 Jan 2017
4. Burley, D.L., et al.: Cybersecurity curricula (2017)

5. Morgan, S.: Cybersecurity job market to suffer severe workforce shortage. CSO (2005). https://www.csoonline.com/article/2953258/it-careers/cybersecurity-job-market-figures-2015-to-2019-indicate-severe-workforce-shortage.html. Accessed 30 Apr 2018
6. Suby, M., Dickson, F.: The 2015 (ISC)^2 Global Information Security Workforce Study. Frost and Sullivan White Paper (2015)
7. Cisco Advisory Services. Mitigating the cybersecurity skills shortage (2015)
8. Fripp, C.: South Africa simply doesn't have enough cybersecurity experts (2017). https://www.htxt.co.za/2016/08/19/south-africa-simply-doesnt-have-enough-cybersecurity-experts/. Accessed 9 Mar 2018
9. McGettrick, A.: Toward curricular guidelines for cybersecurity. In: Report of a Workshop on Cybersecurity Education and Training (2013). https://doi.org/10.1145/2538862.2538990
10. von Solms, S., Futcher, L.: Towards the design of a cybersecurity module for postgraduate engineering studies. In: Proceedings of the International Symposium on Human Aspects of Information Security & Assurance (HAISA 2017), Adelaide, Australia (2017)
11. Newhouse, W., Keith, S., Scribner, B., Witte, G.: National Initiative for Cybersecurity Education (NICE) Cybersecurity Workforce Framework. Special Publication 800–181, NIST2017 (2017)
12. Dove, R., Bayuk, J., Wilson, B., Kepchar, K.: INCOSE System Security Engineering Working Group Charter (2016). https://www.incose.org/docs/default-source/wgcharters/systems-security-engineering.pdf?sfvrsn=cc0eb2c6_8. Accessed 9 Mar 2018
13. Shreyas, D.: Software Engineering for Security: Towards Architecting Secure Software (2001). http://citeseerx.ist.psu.edu/viewdoc/download?doi=10.1.1.3.4064&rep=rep1&type=pdf. Accessed 5 May 2018
14. Haridas, N.: Software Engineering – Security as a Process in the SDLC. SANS Institute InfoSec Reading Room (2007)
15. Tong, A., Sainsbury, P., Craig, J.: Consolidated criteria for reporting qualitative research (COREQ): a 32-item checklist for interviews and focus groups. Int. J. Qual. Health Care **19** (6), 349–357 (2007)
16. Liamputtong, P., Ezzy, D.: Qualitative Research Methods, 2nd edn. Victoria Oxford University Press, Melbourne (2005)
17. Davies, P.H.J.: Spies as informants: triangulation and the interpretation of elite interview data in the study of the intelligence and security services. Politics **21**(1), 73–80 (2001)
18. Aberbach, J.D., Rockman, B.A.: In the Web of Politics: Three Decades of the U.S. Federal Executive. The Brookings Press, Washington, D.C. (2000)
19. Tansey, O.: Process Tracing and Elite Interviewing: A Case for Non-Probability Sampling. PS Polit. Sci. Politics **40**(4), 765–772 (2007)
20. Thomas, D.R.: A general inductive approach for analyzing qualitative evaluation data. Am. J. Eval. **27**(2), 237–246 (2006)
21. ECSA, Qualification Standard for Bachelor of Science in Engineering (BSc (Eng))/ Bachelors of Engineering (BEng): NQF Level 8 4, 1–10 (2014)
22. The Higher Education Qualifications Sub-Framework. Government Gazette No. 36003 of 14 December 2012 (2013)
23. Harvey, W.S.: Strategies for conducting elite interviews. Qual. Res. **11**(4), 431–441 (2011)

A National Certification Programme for Academic Degrees in Cyber Security

Steven Furnell[1](✉), Michael K[2], Fred Piper[3], Chris E[2],
Catherine H2[2], and Chris Ensor[2]

[1] University of Plymouth, Plymouth, UK
sfurnell@plymouth.ac.uk
[2] The National Cyber Security Centre, London, UK
bachelorscertification@ncsc.gov.uk
[3] Codes and Ciphers Limited, Richmond, UK
masterscertification@ncsc.gov.uk

Abstract. With a growing need for cyber security skills, there has been a notable increase in the number of academic degrees targeting this topic area, at both undergraduate and postgraduate levels. However, with a widening and varied choice available to them, prospective students and employers require a means to identify academic degrees that offer appropriate and high-quality education in the subject area. This paper presents a case study of the establishment and operation of a certification programme for academic degrees in cyber security. It describes the means by which appropriate topic themes and subject areas for relevant degrees were identified and defined, leading to a certification programme that addresses degrees in general cyber security as well as notable specialisations including digital forensics and network security. The success of the programme is evidenced by 25 degrees across 19 universities having been certified to date, and a continued response to new calls for certification.

Keywords: Certification · Academic degrees · Bachelor's · Master's
University

1 Introduction

The cyber security domain is widely-recognised as suffering a skills shortage. For example, a 2013 review by the UK's National Audit Office suggested that it could take up to 20 years to bridge the cyber-skills gap [1], while a 2017 study from (ISC)^2 suggested that the workforce gap could reach 1.8 million by 2022 [2]. As a consequence, the UK's National Cyber Security Strategy identifies the need to strengthen cyber security skills as being a key concern, and highlights a series of systemic issues currently contributing to the shortage [3]:

- the lack of young people entering the profession
- the shortage of current cyber security specialists
- insufficient exposure to cyber and information security concepts in computing courses

L. Drevin and M. Theocharidou (Eds.): WISE 2018, IFIP AICT 531, pp. 133–145, 2018.
https://doi.org/10.1007/978-3-319-99734-6_11

– a shortage of suitably qualified teachers
– the absence of established career and training pathways into the profession

It is clear that several of these points relate to academic provision, and the consequent (lack of) supply of qualified graduates to contribute to the discipline. Indeed, further findings from 2017 suggested that only 12% of the UK cyber security workforce is aged under 35 and only 6% of UK companies are hiring appropriately skilled graduates [4]. As such, there is a need to improve the pipeline that higher education can provide, and increase the supply of relevant degree graduates. However, as with security measures themselves, cyber security education is only worthwhile if it is done effectively, and the requirement is more than simply having graduates from degrees that have had superficial coverage of security issues (or worse, had security presented in a manner that is outdated or even incorrect). In this context, it is useful for both prospective students and graduate employers to have a means of identifying credible degrees to match their respective interests and needs. To this end, we present an insight into a successful certification programme that has been introduced by the UK's National Cyber Security Centre (NCSC), including the background and justification for the programme, the design of the certification framework, and some discussion of the experience to date and the related evidence of success.

2 Academic Degrees in Cyber Security

The provision of related degrees in the UK (and indeed internationally) can be traced back to the MSc Information Security, launched by Royal Holloway University of London in 1992 [5]. Since that time, many other degrees have appeared that also target a similar topic space, and the prominence and wider recognition of cyber security in more recent years has arguably served to accelerate this. At the same time, however, it is recognized that some degrees are perhaps more credible than others, and while some are borne out of institutions having a genuine academic presence in the area, others may have been created to capitalize upon the popularity of cyber security. Indeed, one of the main aims of most universities is to offer courses that attract students and one implication of this is that they are attracted to degree titles that receive media attention. Cyber security undoubtedly comes into this category and the growth of degrees that either have the name 'cyber security' or contain cyber security modules has increased dramatically and there are now many alternatives to choose from. For example, at the time of writing, there are in the region of 100 Master's degrees and a slightly larger number of undergraduate degrees in the UK with cyber security or related elements indicated in their titles. There is consequently a need to provide guidance to prospective students and employers on the content and quality of cyber security degrees. Indeed, even where 'security' is in some way present in the degree title, it is not always a guarantee of substantial or sufficient coverage, and an examination of the underlying module/unit titles can sometimes reveal security to be less prominent than might be expected.

Additionally, whilst it may arguably be the case that a university can put together a 'good' syllabus for a degree in cyber security (insofar as they simply need to base it on one that has been published) the quality of the course in practice will depend on the experience of those delivering it. As a baseline, it is therefore important to ensure that the degree content is appropriately matched to the title, *and* that it is supported by a credible academic base from within which to deliver it, in terms of staff expertise and resourcing [6].

In parallel with the growing range of degrees, the UK Cyber Security Strategy identifies a national requirement for "more talented and qualified cyber security professionals" and this in turn leads to an objective "to ensure the sustained supply of the best possible home-grown cyber security talent" [3]. Such recognition was a driver for the NCSC to establish a certification programme for academic degrees in cyber security. In doing so, the aim is to help set the standard for good cyber security higher education in the UK. Related work has previously been undertaken in the USA, with the National Security Agency and Department of Homeland Security granting Centre of Excellence designations to universities demonstrating their ability to map their curricula to defined knowledge areas in cyber defence [7].

3   Establishing a Certification Programme

As indicated above, the certification of degrees offers benefits to both students and employers, and should also help universities themselves in attracting both additional numbers and higher quality students into their degrees. The work to set up the UK programme was initiated in 2013, and began with attention towards postgraduate Master's-level degrees. The postgraduate market was seen to offer the most established range of existing degrees named around security in some form (e.g. computer, cyber, information), as well as more specialised titles addressing areas such as digital forensics and network security. In order to approach the certification process in a structured and phased way, it was decided that an initial programme should be established to address Master's degrees seeking to provide a general and broad foundation in cyber security, and then to follow this with later certifications addressing more specialised degrees, as well as to broaden things out to address undergraduate provision.

The initial work to devise the certification framework began in mid-2013, and a fundamental requirement at the outset was to map out each of the supporting disciplines – specifically the broad domains of cyber security and computer science, as well as the specific of topics such as digital forensics and network/Internet security. Rather than attempt to define each of the areas from scratch, it made sense to look at existing categorisations of the topics, and determine the extent to which they were suitable. A number of options were considered from the security perspective, including the main clauses of ISO 27002 (the international code of practice for information security controls) [8] and the eight domains used by the Common Body of Knowledge within the industry-recognised CISSP certification [9]. However, it was ultimately decided that the most suitable foundation would be the Skills Framework from the Institute of Information Security Professionals [10]. This describes the range of competencies expected of information security professionals, and was developed via collaboration between both private and public-sector organisations, academics, and security leaders. Nonetheless, while it was felt to provide a good starting point, the framework was not designed with the certification of academic degrees in mind, and required some refinement for the intended purpose and the type of content that well-regarded security degrees were already seen to be covering. Specifically, it was felt to have an overly granular emphasis on organisational and managerial aspects of security, while lacking coverage of some key areas on the technical side (e.g. coverage of control systems). This led to some modifications in order to simplify, rebalance, and update the content, and during this period, draft versions of the resulting framework were exposed to external review by a number of stakeholder groups, including government and industry panels, and a wider cross-section of the UK academic community. This ultimately yielded a cyber security subject framework comprising nine Security Disciplines, further sub-divided into 14 Skills Groups, as opposed to ten Disciplines and 32 Groups in the IISP original (the top-level security disciplines remained broadly the same as the IISP set, and also adopted the A-J labelling of the disciplines areas themselves – the notable difference was the omission of IISP discipline G – Audit, Assurance & Review – which for the purposes of the NCSC set had been grouped within discipline A on Information Security Management). The full set of resulting disciplines and associated skills groups is listed in Table 1, and as an aside it can be noted that many of the modifications made for the purposes of the degree certification framework were later fed forward into a revised version of the IISP Skills Framework.

For the computer science theme, the choice was more straightforward, as we were able to draw on the recently published Computer Science Curricula, produced by the Association for Computing Machinery (ACM) and the Institute of Electrical and Electronics Engineers (IEEE) [11]. The subject areas specified within this were adopted for use in the undergraduate certification framework without modification. Consideration was, however, given to the level/depth of coverage that would be expected for each topic, depending upon whether the degree concerned had computer science or cyber security as its main focus, and whether it was at Bachelor's or Integrated Master's level. Table 1 again lists the main subject areas, noting that the ACM specification presents further details, with each area having an associated list of indicative topics coverage.

An assessment of existing postgraduate cyber security degrees in the UK revealed that while the majority would fit the classification of providing a general, broad foundation in the topic, there were nonetheless a range of more specialised degrees to be found. A survey of the market conducted in mid-2014 revealed multiple universities offering degrees in each of the following areas of specialisation:

– computer network and Internet security;
– digital forensics;
– human factors of security;
– secure systems design and development;
– security and risk management.

Of these, digital forensics and network security were the areas in which a more sizeable number of degrees could be identified, with at least six universities offering related degrees at Master's level, and further variants identified in undergraduate provision. As such, these areas were selected as a basis for specialised variants of the certification framework, with digital forensics added in 2014 and the network security

Table 1. Overview of top-level subject areas identified to support degree certification

Theme	Underlying subject areas
Computer Science *(areas adopted from ACM/IEEE)*	1. Algorithms and complexity; 2. Architecture and organisation; 3. Discrete structures; 4. Programming languages; 5. Software development fundamentals; 6. Software engineering; 7. Systems fundamentals; 8. Security fundamentals; 9. Networks (1); 10. Operating systems (1); 11. Human-computer interaction; 12. Information management; 13. Secure programming; 14. Low level techniques and tools; 15. Networks (2); 16. Systems programming; 17. Operating systems (2); 18. Embedded systems; 19. Social issues and professional practice
Cyber Security *(areas adapted from IISP)*	A. Information Security Management (Policy, Strategy, Awareness and Audit; Legal and Regulatory Environment); B. Information Risk Management (Risk Assessment and Management); C. Implementing Secure Systems (Security Architecture; Secure Development); D. Information Assurance Methodologies and Testing (Information Assurance Methodologies; Security Testing); E. Operational Security Management (Secure Operations Management and Service Delivery; Vulnerability Assessment); F. Incident Management (Incident Management; Forensics). H. Business Continuity Management (Business Continuity Planning and Management); I. Information Systems Research (Research); J. Professional Skills
Digital forensics	I. Foundations of Digital Forensics; II. Digital Forensic analysis; III. Digital Forensic practice; IV. An application of Digital Forensics; V. Legal Process; VI. Information security; VII. Evidence handling and management
Computer network and internet security	1. Computer Networks; 2. Cyber Security; 3. Computer Network Security Threats and Attacks; 4. Computer Network Security Operations and Safeguards; 5. Computer Network Security Administration and Management; 6. Information Security and Risk Management

specialisation added in 2016. In both cases, more specific work was required in order to determine and devise the core subject areas that related degrees would be expected to offer, and (unlike the computer science and general cyber security themes) there was no prior work that could be directly adopted or adapted. As such, it was necessary to determine the key subjects for each theme, and the underlying topics within them. This was done in part by looking at good practice already represented within existing degrees, and then by supplementing by further expertise within the project team. The finalised sets of subjects were ultimately agreed through a process that again also involved extensive consultation and feedback with relevant external experts from industry, academia and government. The top-level subject structures are again presented in Table 1.

It is important to note that none of themes within the certification framework sought to prescribe specific syllabi, in terms of what the degrees should actually teach and assess for each topic. Instead each of the subject areas and skills groups were supported by means of indicative topics that degrees would be expected to address if they were to claim that the area was covered. An illustrative example is presented in Fig. 1, expanding upon the Information Security Management discipline area (and its associated skills groups) from within the Cyber Security theme.

Security Discipline	Skills Group	Indicative topic coverage
A. Information Security Management *Principle: Capable of determining, establishing and maintaining appropriate governance of (including processes, roles, awareness strategies, legal environment and responsibilities), delivery of (including polices, standards and guidelines), and cost-effective solutions (including impact of third parties) for information security within a given organisation).* *CESG Knowledge Requirements include:* • *Management frameworks such as ISO 27000 series* • *Legislation such as Data Protection Act* • *Common management Frameworks such as ISO 9000*	**i. Policy, Strategy, Awareness and Audit (A1, A2, A3, A5, G1)**	• The role and function of security policy • Types of security policy • Security standards (e.g. ISO/IEC 27000) • Security concepts and fundamentals • Security roles and responsibilities • Security professionalism • Governance and compliance requirements in law • Third party management • Security culture • Awareness raising methods • Acceptable use policies • Security certifications • Understanding auditability • The internal audit process
	ii. Legal & Regulatory Environment (A6)	• Computer Misuse legislation • Data Protection law • Intellectual property and copyright • Employment issues • Regulation of security technologies

Fig. 1. An extract from the certification guidance, showing a Cyber Security Discipline broken down into Skills Groups and indicative topic coverage

The first call for applications for certification, addressing universities offering general Master's in cyber security was launched in March 2014. The programme was then progressively expanded, with more degree themes being included and broadening the focus beyond solely considering (postgraduate) Master's degrees. At the time of writing, the certification framework as a whole covers ten types of degree, split across Bachelor's, Integrated Master's and Master's levels, as listed in Table 2. For clarification, it is relevant to note that in the UK system Bachelor's and Integrated Master's degrees are undergraduate level degrees of typically three and four years of full-time study respectively (each of which may also be extended by a further year to incorporate an optional or mandatory placement year, depending upon the host institution). Meanwhile, UK Master's degrees are typically one year in duration, noting that the year in this case reflects the full calendar year, rather than incorporating the summer break that is found in traditional undergraduate study.

Table 2. NCSC certification options (as at May 2018).

Degree type	Degree themes/certifications	Typical duration and credits
Bachelor's	Computer Science for Cyber Security	3-years/360 credits
	Computer Science and Cyber Security	
	Computer Science and Digital Forensics	
Integrated Master's	Computer Science for Cyber Security	4-years/480 credits
	Computer Science and Cyber Security	
	Computer Science and Digital Forensics	
Master's	General Cyber Security	1-year/180 credits
	Digital Forensics	
	Computer Science for Cyber Security	
	Computer Network and Internet Security	

While most of the resulting degree themes are self-explanatory from the titles, it is worth making the distinction between what is meant by 'Computer Science *for* Cyber Security' as opposed to 'Computer Science *and* Cyber Security'. The latter case is where a degree (at undergraduate level) provides a comprehensive foundation in core computer science content, and accompanies it by a significant focus upon cyber security topics (with the study balance typically changing from computing towards cyber as the degree progresses). By contrast, the concept of computer science *for* cyber security is intended to reflect a degree (at undergraduate or postgraduate level) that substantially provides candidates with a deep knowledge of computer science topics (particularly system-level aspects – computer science areas 13 to 18 in Table 1), which is likely to serve them well later, in certain lower-level forms of activity in cyber security. Such degrees are still expected to have some specific cyber security coverage, but through a minority of credits and not necessarily to an advanced level. In setting up the undergraduate certification, it was our view that students studying cyber security required a strong foundation in underpinning computer science – hence the adoption of the ACM/IEEE Computing Curricula.

The topic focus (and consequent balance of taught credits) is expected to vary according to the theme and level of the degree concerned. Again, the framework is not prescriptive about the exact number of credits that needs to be associated with the delivery of each topic, but does indicate minimum levels and subject combinations according to the type of degree concerned. This is illustrated in Fig. 2, covering the ten degree types currently eligible for certification. For reference, 10 credits in the UK system is considered to equate to 100 h of study, which may include lectures, tutorials, seminars, practical sessions, assessment, and independent study.

4 The Degree Certification Process and Uptake

The certification process itself involves an extensive application being written for candidate degrees, and a rigorous review of resulting submissions. To gain full certification applications are required to address the following:

Bachelor's Degrees

Computer Science FOR Cyber Security (Pathway A)
- Minimum 270 taught computer science credits.
- At least 240 taught credits map to Computer Science Subject Areas (CSSAs).
- Taught credits cover CSSAs *1-8* and *13-17* in good breadth and depth.
- Dissertation of 20-40 credits relevant to cyber security and within scope of CSSAs *13-18.*

Computer Science AND Cyber Security (Pathway B)
- Minimum 160 taught computer science credits.
- At least 135 taught credits map to CSSAs.
- Taught credits cover CSSAs *1-5* and *6, 9, 10* in good breadth and depth.
- Minimum of 90 taught credits map to Cyber Security Disciplines *A-H.*
- Taught credits cover Cyber Security Skills Groups *i, ii, iii, iv, v* and *x* in good breadth and depth.
- Dissertation of 20-40 credits relevant to cyber security.

Computer Science AND Digital Forensics (Pathway C)
- Minimum 160 taught computer science credits.
- At least 135 taught credits map to CSSAs.
- Taught credits cover CSSAs *1-5, 9, 10* and *6 or 7* in good breadth and depth.
- Minimum of 90 taught credits map to Digital Forensics Subject Areas (DFSAs) *I* to *VII.*
- At least 4 DFSAs covered in good breadth and depth and must include *I* and *II.*
- Dissertation of 20-40 credits within scope of DFSAs *I* to *VII.*

Integrated Master's degrees

Computer Science FOR Cyber Security (Pathway A)
- Minimum 330 taught computer science credits.
- At least 300 taught credits map to Computer Science Subject Areas (CSSAs).
- Taught credits cover CSSAs *1-8* and *11-17* in good breadth and depth.
- Dissertation of 20-50 credits relevant to cyber security and within scope of CSSAs *13-18.*

Computer Science AND Cyber Security (Pathway B)
- Minimum 240 taught computer science credits.
- At least 180 taught credits map to CSSAs.
- Taught credits cover CSSAs *1-7, 9,10* and *12* in good breadth and depth.
- Minimum of 105 taught credits map to Cyber Security Disciplines *A-H.*
- Taught credits cover at least 8 Cyber Security Skills Groups *i* to *xiii* in good breadth and depth.
- Dissertation of 20-50 credits relevant to cyber security.

Computer Science AND Digital Forensics (Pathway C)
- Minimum 240 taught computer science credits.
- At least 180 taught credits map to CSSAs.
- Taught credits cover CSSAs *1-7, 9,10* and *12* in good breadth and depth.
- Minimum of 105 taught credits map to Digital Forensics Subject Areas (DFSAs) *I* to *VII.*
- At least 5 DFSAs covered in good breadth and depth and must include *I* and *II.*
- Dissertation of 20-50 credits within scope of DFSAs *I* to *VII.*

Master's degrees

Computer Science FOR Cyber Security
- At least 70% of taught modules map to Computer Science For Cyber Security Subject Areas *1-7.*
- Taught modules cover Subject Areas *1-3* and three of *4-7* in good breadth and depth.
- Original research dissertation relevant to cyber security and within scope of Subject Areas *1-7,* accounting for 25-45% of credits.

General Cyber Security
- At least 70% of taught modules map to Security Disciplines *A-H.*
- Taught modules cover at least 9 Skills Groups in good breadth and depth.
- Original research dissertation within scope of Security Disciplines *A-H,* accounting for 25-45% of credits.

Digital Forensics
- At least 70% of taught modules map to Digital Forensics Subject Areas *1-7.*
- Taught modules cover all Core Topics in good breadth and depth.
- Original research dissertation within scope of Subject Areas *1-7,* accounting for 25-45% of credits.

Computer Network and Internet Security
- At least 70% of taught modules map to Computer Network and Internet Security Subject Areas *1-6.*
- Taught modules cover all Subject Areas *1-6* in good breadth and depth.
- Original research dissertation relevant to cyber security and within scope of Subject Areas *1-6,* accounting for 25-45% of credits.

Fig. 2. A more detailed breakdown of the distribution and balance of credits between topics areas and levels of study across the different degree types.

1. Evidence of institutional support (a letter from the Vice-Chancellor confirming commitment to the delivery of the degree);
2. Description of the applicant (e.g. the team delivering the degree and the resources to do so, linkage with industry, supported by CVs of key staff);
3. Description of the degree (e.g. the structure and content);
4. Assessment materials (e.g. approach to assessment, supported by examples of coursework that has been set for students and examinations used across the degree);
5. Individual Projects and Dissertations (e.g. the process of assessment and examples of assessed materials);
6. Student numbers and grades achieved (showing the entry and exit profiles of candidates studying on the degree).

Depending upon their preference and the maturity of their degrees, applicants are able to apply for either full or provisional level of certification. To be eligible for the former, a degree must have been running in both the previous and current academic year. Meanwhile, a degree seeking provisional certification does not need to have started yet, or may be running (for the first time) in the current academic year. Provisional applications are judged upon a reduced set of criteria, insofar as there is no assessment of student dissertations or the profile of students entering or graduating from the degree. To give a sense of the extent of resulting applications, those for Master's degrees are typically in the region of 100–150 pages (excluding any dissertation copies), while undergraduate applications can exceed 400 pages due to the greater volume of assessment and degree content materials being included.

All submissions are subject to a panel-based evaluation, encompassing representatives from academia, industry and government with cyber security knowledge and expertise. The panel is led by an independent Panel Chair and panel members typically review 3–5 applications. A full panel typically numbers around 12–15 persons (depending on the number of applications received). Prior to the panel, each submission is read and evaluated by three designated panel members (typically involving one from each of the aforementioned sectors, in all cases avoiding any conflicts of interest with the degree or university under consideration). The applicants are then scored on the basis of areas 2–6 above, according to the level of evidence provided (with 0 for no evidence, through to 4 for excellent evidence. Note that the institutional support letter is not graded, but must be present). Each section must achieve a threshold score of 3 (good evidence) in order for the certification to be awarded. Full certification typically lasts for 5 years, while the provisional level is typically valid for around 2 years (or until the first graduating cohort from the degree).

The response to the launch of the programme was very positive, and has continued to build and sustain interest as awareness has grown in the sector, and as further certification routes have been added to the portfolio. Figure 3 illustrates the overall uptake of the programme since launch, as well as the extent to which applications to date have been successful (noting that there is no quota for the number of certifications that can be awarded, and all applications are assessed entirely on their merits). The 2014 applications were exclusively for the certification of general Master's in cyber security. As the time goes on, however, the underlying data also includes a progressively wider mix of the other degree types and levels, as well as resubmission of applications for some degrees that were unsuccessful in earlier rounds (with many achieving success with their revised and strengthened versions). It should be noted that

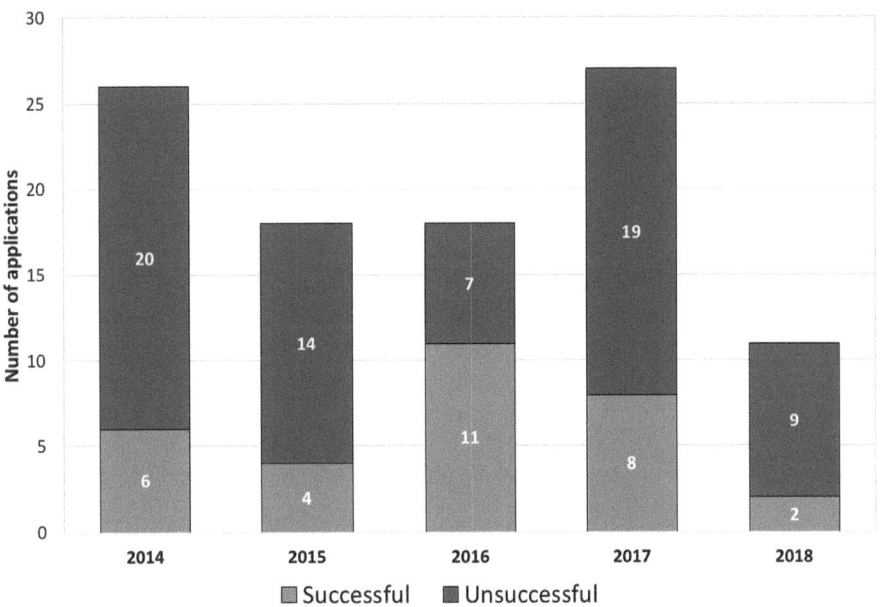

Fig. 3. Overall uptake of the certification programme, indicating the number of successful and unsuccessful applications per annum.

the apparent drop in 2018 is simply because this is based upon only partial data – reflecting the outcome of a Master's certification round, but not including the submissions for a subsequent Bachelor's call (for which the results were not known at the time of writing). Overall application numbers for 2018 are expected to be broadly similar to 2017, based on early indications from the current Bachelor's cycle. There is also a variation in terms of the proportion of degrees applying for full or provisional certification, with more of the applications in the more recent years tending towards the provisional route initially. Nonetheless, the programme has demonstrated a clear impact, and this appears likely to continue as the full range of certifiable degree routes becomes further established.

In addition, a number of further details have been established from the UK's Higher Education Statistics Agency in relation to the 2013/14, 14/15 & 15/16 academic years. Specifically, the number of UK nationals studying a Master's degree in cyber security has shown a healthy year-on-year increase over that period (from 260 to 460). Of these, the percentage studying a certified Master's degree has also shown a healthy increase (from 34% to 51%), so that of those UK nationals who choose to study a Master's in cyber security, the majority now choose a certified degree. This is again indicative of significant positive impact from the programme as a whole, and individual universities have reported positive recruitment effects as a result of gaining the certification.

5   Lessons Learned

With the overall certification and assessment process now having run for several years, it is possible to reflect upon a number of lessons learned. In terms of overall feedback from those directly involved, the assessors and panel chairs involved have consistently confirmed it is a very rigorous and fair process, and that a high bar has been set in terms of degree quality. Consensus on scoring has been good throughout, suggesting that the certifications and underlying criteria have been defined in a suitable manner and are effective in enabling assessors to understand the expected quality and identify whether it exists within the degrees.

The basic structure of the certification and the elements assessed (i.e. considering the academic team, degree content, assessments, dissertations, and student numbers) have also proven effective. Of these, the degree content is probably the most difficult and complex aspect for the panel to consider and evaluate. Assessments have flagged up a number of cases where this is heavily bookwork based and the process has been refined over the years to explicitly indicate that the ratio of bookwork to analysis would not be expected to exceed 60:40 at Master's level. Dissertations have proven very effective in providing an insight into the marking of students' work and provide good evidence of whether the students' work ultimately aligns with what the degree was positioning them to have learned.

The process has also demonstrated that universities are willing and able to benefit from the panel feedback. Over time, a number of submissions that initially failed to achieve the certification have returned in revised form (with associated modifications in terms of factors such as resourcing, content and/or assessment materials), and have then been successful. In these situations, the submissions have been revised in terms of more than just wording and presentation, and it is evident that the feedback has been helpful in guiding the academic teams in refining their degrees and/or enabling them to secure an increased level of support from their institutions.

Overall, it is clear that although the process demands excellence to be successful this has been achieved by a number of universities, and the number is growing.

6   Conclusions

The ongoing need for cyber security skills is likely to drive a corresponding demand for related academic degrees. This in turn creates an associated requirement for students and employers to have a means of identifying relevant and high-quality degrees that match the aspects of cyber security that they are interested in. In this context, the NCSC's certification programme has already made a notable contribution in the UK context. There has been demonstrable uptake of the approach, and feedback suggests that it has served to bring clarity and credibility to the degree landscape. Of course, this does not mean that all uncertified cyber security degrees are lacking credibility, but it *does* mean that those with certification can be trusted. This simplifies matters for industry and employers looking to recruit appropriate graduates.

Moreover, the certification framework is now providing a basis against which new cyber security degrees are being designed. Indeed, the applications for provisional certification suggest an increase in the number of degrees seeking to address cyber security, and the structure of some of those now proposed (particularly at Master's level) has clearly been aided (or even driven) by the availability of the certification standards.

In the years since the certification work was initiated, other initiatives have also emerged that also seek to clarify the expectations of academic degrees in the security domain. A notable example in this context is the CSEC2017 Cybersecurity Education Curriculum [12], which aims to provide comprehensive cybersecurity curricular content at the post-secondary level and results from a two-year joint task force led by the ACM and the IEEE Computer Society, in collaboration with related groups within the Association for Information Systems and the International Federation for Information Processing. Moreover, the certification activity itself sits within a wider portfolio of NCSC-supported activities linked to academia. These also include support for Academic Centres of Excellence in Cyber Security Research, Academic Research Institutes, and Doctoral Studentships (see https://www.ncsc.gov.uk/Academics-and-researchers). Perhaps most notably, since starting the degree certification programme the UK's National Cyber Security Programme has begun to fund a project to identify and describe the foundational knowledge in cyber security – the Cyber Security Body of Knowledge (https://www.cybok.org). This work is being undertaken by a team of UK academics led by the University of Bristol, drawing on the expertise of international cyber security experts as authors and reviewers. The work has identified 19 cyber security Knowledge Areas grouped into 5 main categories: systems security; infrastructure security; software and platform security; human, organisational and regulatory aspects; attacks and defences [13]. Over the next few years, we anticipate that we will increasingly start to use the CyBOK as the reference for defining the content of cyber security degrees. This may lead to different 'flavours' of certified degrees depending on the content pathways chosen through the CyBOK.

Acknowledgements. We would like to thank the team of assessors and Panel Chairs who have worked with us over the past four years and without whom we would not have been able to set up the certification programme.

We would also like to thank Prof. Andy Jones from the University of Hertfordshire for his help in developing the content for Digital Forensics and Computer Network and Internet Security themes.

The data shown in Sect. 4 is Copyright Higher Education Statistics Agency Limited. Neither the Higher Education Statistics Agency Limited nor HESA Services Limited can accept responsibility for any inferences or conclusions derived by third parties from data or other information supplied by HESA Services. Source(s) for Sect. 4: HESA Student Record 2015/16; HESA Student Record 2014/15; HESA Student Record 2013/14; HESA DLHE Record 2015/16; HESA DLHE Record 2014/15; HESA DLHE Record 2013/14; HESA Student Record 2016/17; HESA DLHE Record 2016/17.

References

1. National Audit Office: The UK cyber-security strategy: Landscape review, 12 February 2013. www.nao.org.uk/report/the-uk-cyber-security-strategy-landscape-review/
2. Center for Cyber Safety and Education: 2017 Global Information Security Workforce Study Benchmarking Workforce Capacity and Response to Cyber Risk, Frost & Sullivan Executive Briefing (2017). https://iamcybersafe.org/wp-content/uploads/2017/06/Europe-GISWS-Report.pdf
3. HM government: national cyber security strategy 2016–2021, 1 November 2016. https://www.gov.uk/government/publications/national-cyber-security-strategy-2016-to-2021
4. Cox, J.: UK faces dramatic cyber-security skills 'cliff edge' and is chronically under prepared for hacker attacks, study finds, The Independent, 13 February 2017. https://www.google.co.uk/amp/s/www.independent.co.uk/news/business/news/uk-cyber-security-skills-cliff-edge-under-prepared-hacker-attacks-study-multinationals-government-a7578091.html
5. Martin, K.M., Ciechanowicz, C., Piper, F.C., Robshaw, M.J.B.: Ten years of information security Master's programmes: reflections and new challenges. In: Security Education and Critical Infrastructures: Proceedings of WISE 2003, pp. 215–230. Kluwer (2003)
6. Furnell, S.: Securing a good degree? IISP Pulse, Issue 5, Spring 2011, pp. 6–8 (2011)
7. NSA: National centers of academic excellence in cyber defense, 3 May 2016. https://www.nsa.gov/resources/educators/centers-academic-excellence/cyber-defense/
8. ISO: Information technology – Security techniques – Code of practice for information security controls, ISO/IEC 27002:2013. International Organisation for Standardisation, 1 October 2013. www.iso.org/standard/54533.html
9. (ISC)²: The (ISC)² CBK. https://www.isc2.org/Certifications/CBK#. Accessed 10 May 2018
10. IISP: IISP information security skills framework, V6.3, July 2010. Institute of Information Security Professionals (2010)
11. CS2013: Computer Science Curricula 2013 - Curriculum Guidelines for Undergraduate Degree Programs in Computer Science, 20 December 2013. https://www.acm.org/binaries/content/assets/education/cs2013_web_final.pdf

12. CSEC2017: Cybersecurity Curricula 2017 - Curriculum Guidelines for Post-Secondary Degree Programs in Cybersecurity, Version 1.0 Report, 31 December 2017. https://www. acm.org/binaries/content/assets/education/curricula-recommendations/csec2017.pdf
13. Rashid, A., Danezis, G., Chivers, H., Lupu, E., Martin, A.: Scope for the cyber security body of knowledge, Version 2.0, 10 November 2017. https://www.cybok.org/media/downloads/ CyBOKScopeV2.pdf

Author Index

Zeitfracht Medien GmbH
Ferdinand-Jühlke-Straße 7
99095 Erfurt, Deutschland
produktsicherheit@kolibri360.de